LIVING ON THE CUTTING EDGE

LIVING ON THE CUTTING EDGE

Joshua and the Challenge of Spiritual Leadership

R. KENT HUGHES

CROSSWAY BOOKS • WESTCHESTER, ILLINOIS
A DIVISION OF GOOD NEWS PUBLISHERS

Published by Crossway Books, a division of Good News Publishers, Westchester, Illinois 60153.

Second printing, 1989

Printed in the United States of America

Library of Congress Catalog Card Number 86-72055

ISBN 0-89107-414-7

For my sons
Richard Kent
and
William Carey

TABLE OF CONTENTS

1

PREPARATION FOR SPIRITUAL LEADERSHIP

The study of the Book of Joshua fascinates us for two reasons. The first is historical. Joshua recounts the twenty-five-year story of Israel's victory over the seven nations which occupied the Promised Land. This epic, swashbuckling record begins with the dramatic crossing of the Jordan; it ends a quarter of a century later with Joshua's farewell address and these words: "choose for yourselves today whom you will serve . . . but as for me and my house, we will serve the Lord" (Joshua 24:15). Readers throughout the centuries have been gripped by this intensely graphic, fast-paced historical drama. There is nothing like it—anywhere.

But Joshua's account provides *spiritual enlightenment* as well as historical excitement. Israel's gradual possession of the Promised Land is a paradigm of how we come into further possession of our spiritual riches in Christ. From it we learn the principles of spiritual warfare and of living in faith and obedience. In addition to this primary benefit, we are instructed in many other important areas, such as the holiness of God, the folly of human effort apart from Him, and the principles of spiritual leadership. The study of Joshua promises to be a great spiritual help to all who take the time.

Joshua the Man

Any study of the Book of Joshua must start with a look at the man Joshua, for he did not suddenly appear like a jack-in-the-box at the death of Moses. He was, in fact, *eighty* years old at the time. Scripture divides his life into three periods: forty years in Egypt, forty years in the wilderness with Moses, and twenty-five years in subduing the Promised Land. We will first examine the middle period of preparation under Moses because it provides us with a great subject: *how God readies His people for spiritual leadership*. Joshua successfully succeeded one of the greatest leaders in history, and his preparation can be a valuable lesson to us today. God still prepares His people the same way.

All we know of Joshua's early life in Egypt is that he came from a prominent family in the tribe of Ephraim; his father's name was Nun and his grandfather's name was Elishama (1 Chronicles 7:26, 27). Elishama was captain and head of the tribe of Ephraim (Numbers 1:10; 2:18). Though this is all the Scripture tells us, it provides us with a hint as to why Joshua so quickly rose to such prominence. Numbers 2:18 reveals that his grandfather, Elishama, was still living at the time of the Exodus and therefore marched at the head of his 40,500 people. Quite naturally, his son, Nun, and his grandson, Joshua, also marched with him. Thus Joshua already held a place of prominence.

Moreover, since the camp of Ephraim included the tribes of Manasseh and Benjamin, who were also descendants of Rachel (Numbers 2:18–24), Ephraim was charged with carrying the coffin which contained Joseph's "bones" (no doubt his mummy) from Egypt (Exodus 13:19). Such a situation may well have inclined Joshua to a heroic spirit. We can imagine him, in the prime of his life, proudly marching with his father and aged grandfather alongside Joseph's catafalque, at the head of Ephraim's thousands as the great throng left Egypt for the Promised Land. In Joshua's veins coursed the blood of Joseph. Joshua, no doubt, longed to live up to his remarkable heritage. God, then, had long been at work on Joshua's psyche, preparing him for the great responsibilities to come.[1]

But it is the middle period of Joshua's life, immediately following the Exodus, from which we learn the most about his preparation for spiritual leadership. Here we learn that there were at least seven experiences which shaped Joshua's spiritual leadership. It is as if the Holy Spirit assembled a basic theology of leadership which can be traced simply by looking up Joshua's name as it appears in the Pentateuch. We will consider these experiences in the order that they appear in Scripture. How amazingly wide-ranging and comprehensive they are!

Preparation at Rephidim (Exodus 17:8-16)

Interestingly, the name of Joshua does not appear in the early records of the Exodus, such as the conflict with Pharaoh or the crossing of the Red Sea. The first mention comes after the Amalekites' attack upon the stragglers at Israel's rear in Exodus 17:8, 9:

> Then Amalek came and fought against Israel at Rephidim. So Moses said to Joshua, "Choose men for us, and go out, fight against Amalek. Tomorrow I will station myself on the top of the hill with the staff of God in my hand" (see also Deuteronomy 25:17, 18).

Moses, now into his eighties, took the rod of God with which he had parted the Red Sea and ascended a nearby hill; Joshua, in his fighting prime, took charge of the army. In the ensuing battle, when Moses lifted his hands in intercessory prayer, Israel prevailed. When, due to weariness, he lowered them, Amalek gained the advantage. Soon Aaron and Hur were called to assist Moses, seating him on a stone and standing each at one side to hold his hands upwards. When sunset came, Israel had carried the day.

The lessons for Joshua were clearly manifest. He learned that the real power was not in his sword but in God. No doubt he could have been well-tempted to forget that. He was an instant hero; that night all the campfires sang the name of Joshua. But Joshua kept his feet on the ground. Forever fixed in his mind was the image of Aaron and Hur coming to Moses' side and lifting his hands up to God.

No one attains true spiritual leadership who thinks that his power is his own or that past victories are due to his own genius. The overriding lesson Joshua learned at Rephidim was that the backbone of any work done for God is prayer.

In today's church, those who systematically pray for people and ministry and programs make up the backbone. And in most churches it is the older, experienced saints who understand this best and become the Aarons and Hurs—for life has taught them the importance of prayer. I am convinced beyond any doubt that virtually all advances for Christ come because of believers who understand and practice prayer. E. M. Bounds said of those who have had effective spiritual leadership, "They are not leaders because of brilliancy . . . but because, by the power of prayer, they could command the power of God."[2]

Preparation on Mount Sinai (Exodus 24:9-18)

The next mention of Joshua's name in Scripture comes in Exodus 24:13, in the midst of the text which describes Moses' ascent of Mount Sinai to receive the Law. Verses 9-18 tell us that Moses, Aaron, Nadab, Abihu, and seventy elders of Israel (of whom Joshua was one) were called up the mountain. After climbing some distance and seeing a distant vision of God's glory, the seventy remained behind; Joshua and Moses went further up (v. 13). Here Joshua was with Moses six days when the glorious cloud covered Sinai (v. 15). But on the seventh day Moses went on alone, leaving Joshua by himself on Sinai for forty days (v. 18).

The Sinai experience left its mark on Joshua. His initial vision of God majestically standing over a pavement of sapphire (v. 10), and his subsequent forty days of solitary meditation—while Moses, up in the glowing thundering cloud on Sinai, received the Law—branded his heart with a deep sense of God's glory, holiness, and power. Joshua's vision of God went far beyond the paganism of Egypt and was more exalted than that of his Hebrew contemporaries, as later history would prove.

Even so, our vision of God makes all the difference in life. That was what set King David apart from the rest of the leaders of Israel in his day. Before and during David's teenage years, Israel had fallen from its lofty conceptions of God. The nation's selection of King Saul to rule over them served to hasten their degeneracy, so that, confronted in battle by the Philistines, the Israelites cowered before their armies and their champion—Goliath. To be sure Goliath was awesome. But he was just a man among men. The problem was that the Israelites, having lost their divine perspective, were no longer able to see life's problems in proper view and thus regarded Goliath as an impossible obstacle. But young David retained the divine perspective. Remember his words: "Who is this uncircumcised Philistine that he should defy the armies of the living God?" David didn't measure Goliath; he measured his God.

The same kind of vision is what elevated the Apostle Paul

to his great leadership in the early church. In 2 Corinthians 12:15 he described being caught up into the third heaven, seeing and hearing things beyond words. It was a stupendous spiritual vision. I believe that is what made the difference in his life. That is why, despite a horrible litany of abuses and suffering, he stood true to God and experienced such amazing spiritual leadership.

How important such a vision is to spiritual leadership. It has made the difference in the lives of men and women like Augustine and Hudson Taylor and Mother Teresa. If we desire to lead, we must desire a greater vision of God.

Preparation in the Tabernacle (Exodus 33)

We find another aspect of Joshua's preparation for leadership in Exodus 33, where we glimpse his growing devotion to God. He was serving in the Tabernacle with Moses while the pillar of the cloud towered above the tent. Verse 11 says:

> Thus the Lord used to speak to Moses face to face, just as a man speaks to his friend. When Moses returned to camp, his servant Joshua, the son of Nun, a young man, would not depart from the tent.

Though he was not privileged, like Moses, to speak with God face to face, Joshua was so overcome by His presence that he would not leave the Tabernacle! There is passion in this picture. "Lord, You are so wonderful. I cannot leave this room. I beg You, let me stay."

True spiritual leadership demands a love for the closet, for time alone with God. We cannot name one great leader in the church who did not make personal devotion his top priority. Such were the lives of Bunyan, Wesley, Mueller, Lloyd-Jones, and many other notable men and women of God. One hundred years ago the great C. J. Vaughn said:

> If I wished to humble anyone, I should question him about his prayers. I know nothing to compare with the topic for its sorrowful confessions.[3]

What if Vaughn asked us the question today?

Preparation Within the Camp (Numbers 11:24ff.)

The next mention of Joshua is not as flattering as the others have been:

> So Moses went out and told the people the words of the Lord. Also, he gathered seventy men of the elders of the people, and stationed them around the tent. Then the Lord came down in the cloud and spoke to him; and He took of the Spirit who was upon him and placed Him upon the seventy elders. And it came about that when the Spirit rested upon them, they prophesied. But they did not do it again. But two men had remained in the camp; the name of one was Eldad and the name of the other Medad. And the Spirit rested upon them (now they were among those who had been registered, but had not gone out to the tent), and they prophesied in the camp. So a young man ran and told Moses and said, "Eldad and Medad are prophesying in the camp." Then Joshua the son of Nun, the attendant of Moses from his youth, answered and said, "Moses, my lord, restrain them." But Moses said to him, "Are you jealous for my sake? Would that all the Lord's people were prophets, that the Lord would put His Spirit upon them!" (Numbers 11:24–29).

Joshua had to learn that spiritual leadership and self-promotion are incompatible. Moses knew this—for he was the humblest man on the face of the earth (Numbers 12:3). He refused to let Joshua glorify him.

For Joshua, this was very probably a watershed experience. Had he not been checked here, his "selfless jealousy" for Moses' honor could eventually have made him a narrow, petty man—unfit for leadership. As it turned out, the lesson was well-learned; Joshua never again displayed such smallness, and remained a man who lived only for God's glory.

Unfortunately, the church has not always appropriated this lesson. John Claypool says, in his 1979 Yale Lectures on Preaching, that while in seminary he experienced jealous jockeying for position and that life in the parish ministry has not been much different. In his own words he says:

> I can still recall going to state and national conventions in our denomination and coming home feeling drained and un-

> clean, because most of the conversation in the hotel rooms and the halls was characterized either by envy of those who were doing well or scarcely concealed delight for those who were doing poorly. For did that not mean that someone was about to fall, and would thus create an opening higher up the ladder?[4]

Spiritual leadership excludes this. How much better the example of Charles Simeon, the famous Cambridge preacher. His biographer, Hugh Evan Hopkins, tells us that:

> When in 1808 Simeon's health broke down and he had to spend some eight months recuperating in the Isle of Wight, it fell to Thomason to step into the gap and preach as many as five times on a Sunday in Trinity Church and Stapleford. He surprised himself and everyone else by developing a preaching ability almost equal to his vicar's, at which Simeon, totally free from any suggestion of professional jealousy, greatly rejoiced. He quoted the Scripture, "He must increase; I must decrease," and told a friend, "Now I see why I have been laid aside. I bless God for it."[5]

True spiritual leadership knows nothing of a self-promoting spirit.

Apropos to this truth is the fact that Joshua's regular designation, used several times in the Pentateuch, is Joshua the "servant of Moses." Sometimes the term is rendered "page," "aide," "lieutenant," or "minister," but the title always carries the idea of subservience. Significantly, Joshua remained Moses' servant until his leader died (cf. Exodus 24:13; Numbers 11:28). Though second violin is a difficult instrument to master (much harder than first chair!), Joshua played it well. In fact, he was a virtuoso second fiddle.

True spiritual leaders, like Joshua, can be number two, number three, four, five . . . Jesus, the ultimate Joshua, showed us how.

> For who is greater, the one who reclines at table, or the one who serves? Is it not the one who reclines at table? But I am among you as the one who serves (Luke 22:27).

Those who qualify for spiritual leadership are supportive Joshuas to each other and to all those around.

Preparation in Spying Out the Land (Numbers 13, 14)

We next see Joshua's name in connection with the famous incident of spying out the land. Moses commissioned twelve spies (one from each tribe) to reconnoiter the Promised Land as a prelude to conquest. He appointed Caleb and Joshua as representatives of their respective tribes (13:6, 8). After forty days of covert inspection, the scouts returned. All agreed that the land was bountiful (13:23, 24), but ten of the spies said it could not be conquered because the cities were well-fortified and some of the people were giants (vv. 28, 29). Caleb and Joshua countered that victory was a "piece of cake," a *fait accompli*. Note that the Hebrew of 14:9 literally says, "Do not fear the people of the land, for our bread they are." All they had to do, the two men insisted, was move in (13:30; 14:9). But the rest of Israel sided with the majority, and even tried to stone Joshua and Caleb (14:1-10). The result was God's judgment.

> Surely you shall not come into the land in which I swore to settle you, except Caleb the son of Jephunneh and Joshua the son of Nun. Your children, however, whom you said would become a prey—I will bring them in, and they shall know the land which you have rejected. But as for you, your corpses shall fall in this wilderness. And your sons shall be shepherds for forty years in the wilderness, and they shall suffer for your unfaithfulness, until your corpses lie in the wilderness. According to the number of days which you spied out the land, forty days, for every day you shall bear your guilt a year, even forty years, and you shall know My opposition. I the Lord have spoken, surely this I will do to all this evil congregation who are gathered together against Me. In this wilderness they shall be destroyed, and there they shall die (14:30-35).

For Joshua the lesson was quite clear: the majority is not always right. In fact, it is very often wrong. The men and women God uses have always stood against the flow—Luther, Knox, Fox, Wilberforce, Booth, Carey, Bonhoeffer. We need to remember this. Ours is a day when truth is determined by consensus, when justice is struck by a five-four vote, when "everybody is doing it" has become the pervasive rationale for behavior, when Jefferson's fear of the tyranny of the majority is a reality. Spiritual leaders do not necessarily go with the majority opinion.

In this incident, we see Joshua coming of age. Moses saw it too, and beautifully changed his name to the name by which we know him, Joshua: "These are the names of the men whom Moses sent to spy out the land; but Moses called Hoshea the son of Nun, Joshua" (Numbers 13:16). Hoshea meant "salvation," but Joshua means "Jehovah (Yahweh) is salvation." Moses thus testified to Joshua's development—"Here is the man who is going to save Israel." His name told what he was going to do. It is the name God's Son took when He came into the world. "And you shall call His name Jesus, for it is He who will save His people from their sins" (Matthew 1:21).

Preparation in His Commissioning (Numbers 27:18-23)

Joshua had come a long way in those forty years of wandering. So it was on the plain of Moab, when, according to Numbers 26:65, "not a man was left of them, except Caleb the son of Jephunneh, and Joshua the son of Nun," that the time came for Joshua's commissioning.

> So the Lord said to Moses, "Take Joshua the son of Nun, a man in whom is the Spirit, and lay your hand on him; and have him stand before Eleazar the priest and before all the congregation; and commission him in their sight. And you shall put some of your authority on him, in order that all the congregation of the sons of Israel may obey him" (Numbers 27:18-20).

Notice that the Spirit, capital S—the Holy Spirit—was upon and in Joshua. He had the *sine qua non* for all spiritual leadership. J. Oswald Sanders says:

> Spiritual leadership is a matter of superior spiritual power, and it can never be self-generated. There is no such thing as a self-made spiritual leader.[6]

The New Testament agrees:

> But select from among you, brethren, seven men full of the Spirit . . . and they chose Stephen, a man full of faith and the Holy Spirit . . . (Acts 6:3, 5).

When all is said and done, spiritual leadership is the sovereign work of the Holy Spirit.

W. E. Sangster, the great Methodist preacher who galvanized England with his powerful preaching during World War II, wrote in a private manuscript discovered after his death:

> This is the will of God for me.
> I did not choose it. I sought to escape
> it. But it has come.
> Something else has come too. A sense of
> certainty that God does not want me only
> for a preacher. He wants me also for a leader—
> a leader in Methodism.
> I feel a commissioning to work under God for the
> revival of this branch of His Church—
> careless of my own reputation; indifferent
> to the comments of older and jealous men.
> I am thirty-six. If I am to serve God in
> this way, I must no longer shrink from
> the task—but do it.
> I have examined my heart for ambition. I am
> certain it is not there. I hate the
> criticism I shall evoke and the painful
> chatter of people. Obscurity, quiet browsing
> among books, and the service of simple people
> is my taste—but by the will of God, this
> is my task. God help me.[7]

We must equip ourselves as best we can, but when all is said and done, we must understand and believe that without the Holy Spirit nothing will happen. Spiritual leadership rests on the anointing of the Holy Spirit.

Deuteronomy records another commissioning, much the same, and God's words are beautiful:

> Be strong and courageous, for you shall bring the sons of Israel into the land which I swore to them, and I will be with you (31:23).

And with that Moses began to sing—his final song.

Preparation Through the Death of Moses (Deuteronomy 34:7, 8)

Only one thing remained in Joshua's preparation: the death of Moses.

> Now Moses went up from the plains of Moab to Mount Nebo, to the top of Pisgah, which is opposite Jericho. And the Lord showed him all the land, Gilead as far as Dan, and Naphtali and the land of Ephraim and Manasseh, and all the land of Judah as far as the Western Sea, and the Negev and the Plain in the valley of Jericho, the city of palm trees, as far as Zoar. Then the Lord said to him, "This is the land which I swore to Abraham, Isaac, and Jacob, saying 'I will give it to your descendants'; I have let you see it with your eyes, but you shall not go over there." So Moses the servant of the Lord died there in the land of Moab, according to the word of the Lord. And He buried him in the valley in the land of Moab, opposite Beth-peor; but no man knows his burial place to this day. Although Moses was one hundred and twenty years old when he died, his eye was not dim, nor his vigor abated. So the sons of Israel wept for Moses in the plains of Moab thirty days; then the days of weeping and mourning for Moses came to an end. Now Joshua the son of Nun was filled with the spirit of wisdom, for Moses had laid his hands on him; and the sons of Israel listened to him and did as the Lord had commanded Moses (Deuteronomy 34:1-9).

Moses was the greatest spiritual leader that Israel ever had, far greater than Joshua. The transition from Moses to Joshua was like going from poetry to prose. But Moses was dispensable. Joshua learned that *no one is indispensable.*

What a truth for us all—for me, for my associates, for the Body of Christ. God does not need us; He can use donkeys if

He wants. But He does use us. Let us glory in God. Let us glory that He uses us. Let us never glory in ourselves.

Let's bring what we have learned about preparation for spiritual leadership together:

> Moses' outstretched hands teach us that spiritual power does not come through human power, but through prayer.
>
> Joshua's experience on the mountain demonstrates that a great vision of God is indispensable for spiritual leadership.
>
> Joshua's refusal to leave the Tabernacle shows the necessity of heart-devotion for spiritual leadership.
>
> Moses' reproof of Joshua's protective jealousy indicates the necessity of excluding self-glorification. His name, "servant of Moses," beautifully tells us that a spiritual leader plays a good second fiddle.
>
> Joshua's spy experience taught him that the majority report is not always the way to go.
>
> His ordination illustrates the necessity of the Holy Spirit for true leadership.
>
> Moses' death shows that no one is indispensable.

When God wants to drill a man
    And thrill a man
    And skill a man,
When God wants to mold a man
    To play the noblest part;
When He yearns with all His heart
    To create so great and bold a man
That all the world shall be amazed,
    Watch His methods, watch His ways!
How He ruthlessly perfects
    Whom He royally elects,
How He hammers him and hurts him,
    And with mighty blows converts him
Into trial shapes of clay which
    Only God understands;
While his tortured heart is crying
    And he lifts beseeching hands!

How He bends but never breaks
    When his good He undertakes;
How He uses whom He chooses
    And with every purpose fuses him;
    By every act induces him
To try His splendor out—
    God knows what He's about.[8]

Footnotes

1. See William Garden Blaikie, *The Book of Joshua* (A. C. Armstrong and Son, 1903), p. 23.
2. Oswald Sanders, *Spiritual Leadership* (Chicago: Moody, 1967), quoting E. M. Bounds, *Prayer and Praying*.
3. Sanders, p. 75.
4. John R. Claypool, *The Preaching Event* (Waco, Tex.: Word, 1980), p. 68.
5. Hugh Evan Hopkins, *Charles Simeon of Cambridge* (Grand Rapids: Eerdmans, 1977), p. 111.
6. Sanders, p. 20.
7. Paul Sangster, *Doctor Sangster* (London: Epworth Press, 1962), p. 109.
8. Sanders, p. 141.

2

THE DIVINE CHARGE
Joshua 1:1-9

With the death of Moses, everything fell on Joshua's shoulders. For four decades he and all Israel had depended upon Moses. And now it was all on him! Knowing as he did the history of his rebellious people, and knowing as he intimately knew the greatness of Moses, Joshua may have been a bit daunted by his new responsibility. If he was, however, the Scripture does not record it. He appears to have received the leadership without remonstrance.

His task was monumental. He had the formidable military assignment of conquering the seven nations which occupied the Promised Land, and then dividing it up fairly among his people. On top of that, he took on the even more challenging task of setting them on the right course spiritually. William Blaikie of Edinburgh put it this way:

> To conquer the country required but the talent of a military commander; to divide the country was pretty much an affair of trigonometry; but to settle them in a higher sense, to create a moral affinity between them and their God, to turn their hearts to the covenant of their fathers, to wean them from their old idolatries and establish them in such habits of obedience and trust that the doing of God's will would become to them a second nature—here was the difficulty of Joshua.[1]

It was a herculean task. Now Joshua was to justify his name. He was to show himself worthy to be called "Jehovah's salvation"—Jesus!

Joshua was in charge. Only one thing remained: God's final instructions, His charge, given in the first nine verses of Joshua 1. It consists of three commands and the promises which result from obedience to each of them. The first command, in verse 2, is to "cross over the Jordan." The second, in verse 6, says "Be strong and courageous." And the third, in verse 7, charges, "Be careful to do according to all the law which Moses My servant commanded you." God's advice to Joshua is transferable to all who would seek to wage successful spiritual warfare and further enjoy the riches of God.

The First Command to Joshua and Its Promises (1:2-5)

God first commanded Joshua to cross the Jordan River. Verses 1 and 2 give this charge in full:

> Now it came about after the death of Moses the servant of the Lord that the Lord spoke to Joshua the son of Nun, Moses' servant, saying, "Moses My servant is dead; now therefore arise, cross this Jordan, you and all this people, to the land which I am giving to them, to the sons of Israel."

It was a fearful order. The fifteenth verse of chapter 3 tells us that the Jordan was in flood stage. The actual river bottom, about one hundred feet wide, forms the bottom of a wider trough called the Ghor which ascends up the slopes of the valley.[2] The river had swollen, filling the Ghor and probably more—making it impassable. For modern armies, such situations are very difficult; for the Israelites, it was a physical impossibility. And God gave no hint of how to do it.

Moreover, Joshua knew that crossing the Jordan meant throwing down the gauntlet. It was a declaration of war—a fight to the finish. Joshua knew that as soon as he crossed the Jordan, the enemies would assemble and fight with the tenacity typical of those fighting for home and hearth. All seven nations would muster their bravest forces. The giants of Anak would come running. Nor would the struggle end in a day, as it had with the Amalekites. As it turned out, the days were not long enough for the battles; when the longest day ended, Joshua still had his sword in his hand. Joshua was like the knights who slept in their armor. His sword became nicked and blunted with use. To top it all off, he was not taking a real, unified army into Canaan, but a mixed multitude of soldiers, as well as women and children whose fathers had proved unfaithful time and time again.

Think of the pressure which came with his leadership. No doubt it affected all his waking moments—and even his sleep. Such pressures have universal effects, as evidenced in the dreams of the man under whom I spent nine years as a pastor. As his wife tells it, she awoke one night to find her husband asleep on his elbows and knees at the foot of the bed. His arms were cupped as if he were holding something, and he was muttering. She said, "What on earth are you doing?" Still asleep, he replied, "Shh, I'm holding a pyramid of marbles together, and if I move, they are all going to fall down." That is a classic pastor's dream! Joshua was under immense pressure, and it could have paralyzed him. Calvin wisely comments:

> But as the most valiant, however well-provided, are apt to halt or waver when the period of action arrives, the exhortation to Joshua to make ready forthwith for the expedition was by no means superfluous.[3]

God told Joshua to get going, to take the first step.

In any challenging venture, the first step is always the hardest. The most difficult words in a term paper are the opening sentences; getting the ink on the page seems impossible. The most difficult "hit" in a football game is the first hit. This general principle holds even more strongly in spiritual matters. In confronting an errant brother, the hardest words are the first you speak. The most difficult step in a new work of faith is the first. Perhaps the most difficult words you will ever utter are the initial words as you share your faith with your neighbor or business acquaintance. But God's command to Joshua brings wisdom to us today: if God tells you to take the first step, do it! Learning to take that step is the key to possessing many of the riches Christ has for you. Are there some steps you need to take? Do you need to cross some Jordans?

This great step had its benefits, listed in verses 3 and 4. First, in verse 4, God said:

> From the wilderness and this Lebanon, even as far as the great river, the river Euphrates, all the land of the Hittites, and as far as the Great Sea toward the setting of the sun, will be your territory.

God's ultimate plan included all the land specified within the ample boundaries. But first the Israelites were to subdue the smaller area which lay directly before them, an area which already had been consecrated many centuries before by the residence of Abraham, Isaac, and Jacob. If they were faithful and consolidated this narrower territory, they would succeed to the greater boundaries. It is a matter of record that, while they did conquer the smaller area under Joshua's leadership, Israel did not, in fact, expand to the greater territory promised. They fell short because, despite their great victories, the people had notable lapses of faith and accepted compromises. Only in the time of Israel's greatest territorial expansion under David and Solomon did the nation nearly fill the boundaries God set.

The reward was generous and inviting: "Every place on which the sole of your foot treads, I have given it to you." That is exactly what happened, and no more. If the people of Israel, through greater faith and fight, had walked further, more land would have been theirs.

The paradigm holds for our day: when God calls us to take the first step, to cross the Jordan, in a task which He has ordained, He expects us to follow it with further steps of faith. Time and time again His children have taken the first and most difficult step, but have failed to take further steps which would carry them on to full possession and power. This happens repeatedly with churches and Christian organizations, whose initial leadership is capable of great steps of faith, but who, with time, will only take cautious, metered, pre-insured baby steps. And they never expand to the great ministry that God had laid out for them. This is equally true for individual Christians. Some of us have taken great steps, but we must *continue* to take great steps and to claim more land.

For those, like Joshua, who are willing to take the big step and follow it with more faithful steps, God extends some further promises, as we see in verse 5:

> No man will be able to stand before you all the days of your life. Just as I have been with Moses, I will be with you; I will not fail you or forsake you.

God guaranteed Joshua that none of his enemies would withstand him. No son of Anak, no giant like Og, the King of Bashan, would prevail. Moreover, his enemies would not even be able to obtain a "draw." The success promised to Joshua was greater than the greatest of world conquerors has managed to secure. Nothing could stop Joshua as he took the steps ordered by God. The promise remains true for us today. If we will take those steps as ordered by God, if we follow God, then no one and nothing will be able to stand before us.

God defined what He meant with an example well known to Joshua: "Just as I have been with Moses, I will be with you." God had been with Moses when he withstood the mightiest monarch with the mightiest armies on earth, and Moses defeated him again and again. God was with Moses when he prevailed over nature and called forth water from the rock, cured his sister's leprosy, and brought down bread from heaven. What a testimony Moses' life was to the presence and power of God. What assurance God's words, "just as I have been with Moses," brought to Joshua!

The final line of verse 5, which says, "I will not fail you or forsake you," can be translated, "I will not drop you or forsake you."[4] The writer of Hebrews quotes this, saying, "I WILL NEVER DESERT YOU, NOR WILL I FORSAKE YOU," and then adds, "so that we may confidently say, 'THE LORD IS MY HELPER, I WILL NOT BE AFRAID. What shall man do to me?'" (Hebrews 13:5, 6). The charge comes to Joshua, and to all who want to wage successful spiritual warfare and enjoy the riches of God, to take the big step—to cross the Jordan—and the rewards are unparalleled. Every place your God-directed steps lead you will be yours. Nothing will withstand you. God will be with you and will not forsake you.

The Second Command to Joshua and Its Promises (1:6-9)

The second imperative in God's charge to Joshua is found in verses 6 and 9, where he was commanded to be brave.

> Verse 6: Be strong and courageous, for you shall gain this people possession of the land which I swore to their fathers to give them.
>
> Verse 9: Have I not commanded you? Be strong and courageous! Do not tremble or be dismayed, for your God is with you wherever you go.

Here the command and promises intertwine. God informed Joshua of his duty to know the presence and the power in him, and thus be strong and courageous. He was to measure the strength at his back against the weakness confronting him, and then act courageously. This Joshua did! He never backed away from anything. Though his people repeatedly let him down, Joshua's name became synonymous with courage.

Courage is absolutely essential for those who would serve God and know His riches in this life. Jesus is the great example here. Jesus was a Joshua. Humanly speaking, He could not have accomplished His mission without His personal courage. Alexander Maclaren says,

> Neither [Joshua] the conqueror of the . . . material land of promise nor the Redeemer who has won everlasting heaven for our portion could do their work without the heroic side of human excellence. . . .[5]

Jesus heroically set His face as a flint toward Jerusalem—and His death. He is, in the words of Isaiah 9:6, *El Gibbor,* the mighty hero God! Courage was a major ingredient of people like Stephen, Martin Luther, John Knox, and Eric Liddell. In our own recent history, it was the hallmark of Martin Niemoller, who, standing before an irate Hitler in 1934, was told, "You confine yourself to the church. I'll take care of the German people!" Pastor Niemoller replied,

> Herr Reichskanzler, you said just now: "I will take care of the German people." But we too, as Christians and churchmen, have a responsibility towards the German people. That responsibility was entrusted to us by God, and neither you nor anyone in this world has the power to take it from us.[6]

For Joshua, who stood on the edge of the Promised Land, the exhortation to be brave was not superfluous—and neither is it to us. Just as we have seen regarding prayer, we can search the millennia of church history without finding a single individual who did great things for God and knew His richness, but had no courage. Without courage we will never become what we are supposed to be.

> But I fear not, nay, I fear not
> the thing to be done;
> I am strong with the strength
> of my lord the Sun:
> How dark, how dark soever the
> race that must needs be run,
> I am lit with the Sun.[7]

The Third Command to Joshua and Its Promises (1:7, 8)

The third and final command of Joshua's marching orders had to do with the Law, God's teaching,[8] and is given in verses 7 and 8:

> Only be strong and very courageous, to be careful to do according to all the law which Moses My servant commanded you; do not turn from it to the right or to the left, so that you may have success wherever you go. This book of the law shall not depart from your mouth, but you shall meditate on it day and night, so that you may be careful to do according to all that is written in it; for then you will make your way prosperous and then you will have success.

God commanded Joshua to *meditate* on the divine writings. The word suggests an almost inaudible murmur.[9] The words of God were to be chewed, swallowed, and digested so that they became part of his thoughts and actions.[10] Joshua was an immensely busy man with greater responsibilities than any of us will ever know, but God commanded him to spend a great portion of his time in meditation over His Word. Meditation is for the person with great responsibilities. The Book of the Law must not depart from his mouth, from his speaking; he was to teach, warn, and encourage from God's Word. This he did, as Joshua 8:34, 35 makes so beautifully clear:

> There was not a word of all that Moses had commanded which Joshua did not read before all the assembly of Israel with the women and the little ones and the strangers who were living among them (cf. Jeremiah 1:9; 15:6; and Ezekiel 2:8—3:3).

Not only did he meditate on God's Word and speak it, but he was called to obey the command "to do according to all the law" which Moses gave him. Joshua had walked with Moses for forty years, but God did not tell Joshua to "try and remember what Moses taught you." Rather, He charged Joshua to immerse himself in the Book, meditating on it, speaking it, and doing it.

It is of no small significance that God so emphatically called Joshua and Israel to the Word as they stood poised on the Jordan. Those who aspire to do anything for God and experience the richness He desires for them must be people of the Word! Deuteronomy 17:18, 19 uses very similar words in instructing all the Hebrew kings. David charged Solomon, saying,

> I am going the way of all the earth. Be strong, therefore, and show yourself a man. And keep the charge of the Lord your God, to walk in His ways, to keep His statutes, His commandments, His ordinances, and His testimonies, according to what is written in the law of Moses, that you may succeed in all that you do and wherever you turn (1 Kings 2:2, 3).

The "great ones" of our times have taken this to heart. I know of some who have read the Bible a hundred times. I have heard of those who have done so a hundred and fifty times. It is said that George Mueller did it two hundred times. David

Livingston read it four times in succession while he was detained in a jungle town.[11] Spurgeon said, "A Bible which is falling apart usually belongs to someone who is not." William Evans, who pastored College Church (Wheaton, Illinois) in the early part of this century had, according to Henrietta Mears, memorized the entire Bible in the *King James* and the New Testament in the *American Standard Version*.[12] Billy Graham says that his medical missionary father-in-law, Nelson Bell, made it a point

> to rise every morning at 4:30 and spend from two to three hours in Bible reading. He didn't use that time to read commentaries or write; he didn't do his correspondence or any of his other work. He just read the Scriptures every morning, and he was a walking Bible encyclopedia. People wondered at the holiness and the greatness in his life.[13]

We should all take this command to heart. If you don't take time to read and meditate, you SHOULD! Busyness is no excuse. Students, who, at a formative time in life, are studying many of the great works of Western civilization, should be reading the Bible—the greatest of them. The business person and the housewife alike ought to spend a good portion of time getting to know God's Word. J. I. Packer said, "Theology is great." Then he named some of the great theologians. But he said, "The most important thing of all is simply to know your Bible." We need to be people of the Word.

But this command also carries its own rewards: ". . . you will have success" (v. 7); ". . . then you will make your way prosperous, and then you will have success" (v. 8). "Success" here means in the Hebrew "to be prudent" or "to act circumspectly." In the religious and ethical sense, it means someone who lets himself and his life be guided by God.[14] Joshua had this kind of success and prosperity. He experienced hardship. Sometimes he failed. But his way was prudent and wise—thus successful. These verses promise, not material success, but success and prosperity in the tasks to which God has called us. What a wonderful, wonderful promise it is! Let us be people of the Word.

In conclusion, recall Ecclesiastes 9:11, where the writer

gives us a pessimistic view of life which does not take God into consideration:

> I again saw under the sun that the race is not to the swift, and the battle is not to the warriors, and neither is bread to the wise, nor wealth to the discerning, nor favor to men of ability; for time and chance overtake them all.

Life often looks this way from ground level. We can never tell what is going to happen. Sometimes the swift win the race; other times, time and chance overtake them. That is the way it is in war and wealth. But this is not true for the believer! It was not true for Joshua, and it is not true for those who follow in his stead and obey the three commands of his final orders—the commands which call for the submission of our wills, characters, and minds to God. Psalm 31:15 says our times are in His hand.

> We must attune our wills with His so that we are willing to take the big step, to cross our Jordans, and then to keep treading out the territory He has for us.
>
> We must knit our characters with the integrity of strength and courage.
>
> We must devote our minds to God's Word. When this happens, we possess the land; no one stands before us; God is with us as He was with Moses; He never leaves us or forsakes us; and we have true success wherever we go.

Footnotes

1. William Gordon Blaikie, *The Book of Joshua* (A. C. Armstrong and Son, 1903), p. 67.
2. M. H. Woudstra, *The Book of Joshua* (Grand Rapids: Eerdmans, 1981), p. 58.
3. John Calvin, *Commentaries on the Book of Joshua* (Grand Rapids: Baker, 1984), p. 26.
4. John J. Davis, *Conquest and Crisis: Studies in Joshua, Judges, and Ruth* (Grand Rapids: Baker, 1976), p. 30.
5. Alexander Maclaren, *Expositions of Holy Scripture: Deuteronomy, Joshua,* Vol. 2 (Grand Rapids: Baker, 1974), p. 93.

6. Dietmar Schmidt, *Pastor Niemoller,* trans. Lawrence Wilson (New York: Doubleday, 1959), p. 94.
7. Sidney Lanier, quoted by Clarence Macartney, *Macartney's Illustrations* (Nashville: Abingdon, 1946), p. 78.
8. E. John Hamlin, *Inheriting the Land* (Grand Rapids: Eerdmans, 1983), p. 6, says that Joshua ". . . understood it to include both law and story. For this reason we do not use 'law' to translate it, but rather 'God's Covenant Teaching' or simply 'God's teaching.'"
9. Woudstra, p. 63.
10. Hamlin, p. 6.
11. Blaikie, p. 65.
12. E. M. Baldwin, *Henrietta Mears and How She Did It* (Ventura, Calif.: Regal, n.d.), p. 148.
13. This message was delivered at the Congress on Discipleship and Evangelism (CODE '76), a gathering of fifteen hundred young people during the Greater San Diego Billy Graham Crusade, August, 1976.
14. Woudstra, p. 63.

3

THE SCARLET CORD
Joshua 2:1-24

The long preparations for the conquest of the Promised Land had now come to an end. The older faithless generation had perished in the wilderness. God had buried Moses in a secret place in one of the valleys of Moab, and had given Joshua his final charge. Only two tasks remained: to spy out the land, and to have the people of Israel spiritually consecrate themselves to the great work. Verses 1-3 describe the spies' mission:

> Then Joshua the son of Nun sent two men as spies secretly from Shittim, saying, "Go, view the land, especially Jericho." So they went and came into the house of a harlot whose name was Rahab and lodged there. And it was told the king of Jericho, saying, "Behold, men from the sons of Israel have come here tonight to search out the land." And the king of Jericho sent word to Rahab, saying, "Bring out the men who have come to you, who have entered your house, for they have come to search out all the land."

This reconnaissance was supremely perilous because Jericho was a walled city situated in an open valley. Furthermore, its inhabitants, the Amorites, were on the lookout. The ominous presence of the Israelites at the Jordan made them suspicious of everyone. No doubt the spies carefully disguised themselves, discarding anything characteristically Hebrew, and did their best to appear Canaanite-Amorite in clothing and accent. Likewise, they approached with great caution. The Jordan was flooding (3:15). So they probably traveled to the north where the fords were easier, then turned southwest to enter Jericho from the west side. This was advantageous because they would have the cover of the caves in the mountains west of Jericho, and the king would be less likely to detect a spy mission from that side.[1]

Apparently unnoticed, they slipped through Jericho's gates, and, in a studied attempt to "get lost" in the city, sought hiding in the house of a prostitute named Rahab. Staying in such a place was characteristic of traveling merchants, and the spies hoped to remain undetected there. The ploy failed on two points. First, someone saw them enter Jericho and followed them to Rahab's establishment. Second, the prostitute immediately discerned their identity. Things were not looking up.

From all appearances they were doomed. The king was calling for them. They could not retreat back into the city. And if they jumped through the window, horsemen would run them down on the plains. Obviously, their time had come—except for one totally unexpected thing—the faith and good works of the prostitute. God's men were saved by the proprietess of a bordello, a woman who sold her body for money, who submitted to any man who crossed her doorway. The New Testament is clear; she was a *pornee,* a prostitute (see James 2:25 and Hebrews 11:31). So unanticipated, and so extraordinary, was her courageous faith that she is included in the "hall of faith" in Hebrews 11, along with the likes of Abraham, Moses, Enoch, David, and Samuel.

This faith, a *prostitute's faith,* is an example for all who would have true faith. It has three important components: the works which demonstrate it, its nature and development, and its wonderful benefits.

Faith's Work

Verses 4 and 5 make clear a very awkward truth: Rahab's first work of faith was a lie.

> But the woman had taken the two men and hidden them, and she said, "Yes, the men came to me, but I did not know where they were from. And it came about when it was time to shut the gate, at dark, that the men went out; I do not know where the men went. Pursue them quickly, for you will overtake them."

Actually Rahab told three lies in one: first, she said she did not know where they came from; secondly, she said they had gone; and finally, she said she did not know where they were. So here we have it—a lie is the first fruit of Rahab's faith! Does this mean it is okay to lie under certain situations? I personally do not think so, though some highly respected theologians do.[2] I agree with Calvin, who comments on Rahab's deception:

> As to the falsehood, we must admit that though it was done for a good purpose, it was not free from fault. For those who hold what is called a dutiful lie to be altogether excusable, do not sufficiently consider how precious truth is in the sight of God. Therefore, although our purpose be to assist our brethren, to consult for their safety and relieve them, it never can be lawful to lie, because that cannot be right which is contrary to the nature of God. And God is truth. . . . On the whole, it was the will of God that the spies should be delivered, but He did not approve of saving their lives by falsehood.[3]

The Scriptures do, indeed, record the lies of saints like Abraham (Genesis 12:10-20), but they never approve of them. The Scriptures uniformly condemn falsehood and call us to truth. Moreover, the life of Christ, our model *par excellence,* gives us a supreme example of truthfulness. Christ never lied or deceived anyone. And as members of His Body, we must live according to His example.

Nevertheless, Rahab's lie was a stupendous act of true faith. It, and the subsequent actions (vv. 15 and 16) when she assisted the spies in their escape through her window and cleverly advised them to hide three days in the hill country, put her life in great danger. In fact, if the king had gotten wind of it, her death would have been long and terrible. Her faith was great—and deserves the status it has been given. We must consider Rahab's lie in terms of her culture and lowly profession. She had no knowledge of the revelation given to Israel. She was in the outermost circle of God's people, just touching the boundary. We can be sure that the ethics of truth and falsehood never crossed her mind. It never occurred to her that she could be doing any wrong. Her great lie was a great work of faith!

The lessons she leaves us are many, but one we should particularly keep in mind is that we must be sympathetic and patient with the character of converts from our post-Christian culture. John Newton, the author of "Amazing Grace," composer of the Olney hymns, and the early leader of the evangelical movement in the Church of England, continued to participate in the slave trade for over a year after he became a believer.[4] Faith and sin mingled in his life.

Dick Day, who, along with Josh McDowell and Paul Lewis, runs the Julian Center in San Diego—a Christian organization which helps believers approach their faith holistically—tells that he first came to Christ in the midst of a hard-drinking business environment. He says that in order to get up enough courage to share his newfound faith with his boss, he had to have six martinis. Rahab would understand this completely. Often sins are salted with faith, and God finds faith where we do not (and often cannot) see it. We should be slow to judge sin and quick to perceive faith.

The classic symbol which revealed Rahab's great faith was the scarlet cord she hung from her window on the wall of Jericho. Verses 18-20 record how the two spies promised her safety if she would display that cord in her window. They promised that everyone in the house would be safe if the red cord was in place. Rahab's faith produced this saving work. Verse 21 says:

> And she said, "According to your words, so be it." So she sent them away, and they departed; and she tied the scarlet cord in the window.

This tells us that Rahab's faith, though incipient and uninformed, was completely trusting. If the Israelites failed to return and conquer the city, she would soon be found out. The gathering of her family into her home would be interpreted for what it was. Someone would talk. And she and her kin would go to their graves uncomfortably. Rahab completely believed that judgment was coming and that salvation awaited her; so she displayed the red cord.

Here a word about the scarlet cord is in order. Too much has been made of it, as the history of interpretation reveals. Some of the Church Fathers thought that the red cord was a symbol of the blood of Christ and that Rahab was a symbol of the church because she obtained safety for her family.[5] This type of allegorization has been popular in recent years. My wife recalls listening, as a little girl, to a flannelgraph story in which the spies supposedly escaped down a red cord—which, of course, they did not, for the cord was simply hung in the window as a symbol. After this she also saw the teacher stretch the cord out as a symbol of the bloodline of Christ, which it was not.

Now, having said this, I would like to suggest that there is a direct connection with the Passover, which occurred forty years earlier. Then, you will remember, the Israelites were commanded to gather all their family into the house (just as Rahab did) and paint lamb's blood around the door, so that when the death angel came and saw the blood, all inside would be spared alive (Exodus 12:21-23). What happened with Rahab parallels this closely, and it seems likely that the spies (though not Rahab) were quite aware of the symbolism. In both cases the red upon the door or the window evidenced the faith of those inside.

> When the children of Israel were about to leave Egypt, they were given the blood of the Passover Lamb under which to be safe. When the people were about to enter the land, they were met by a different, but parallel sign—a red cord hanging from the window of a believer.[6]

Rahab's faith was great in its trust.

By secluding her family in her home and patiently awaiting the outcome, Rahab revealed her faith. Everything rested upon it. She stood alone against the whole of her culture, something few of us in our Western culture know anything about. She, like Moses before, saw the unseen when no one else did (Hebrews 11:27). By faith she separated herself from her people. She believed!

The Apostle James, in the second chapter of his letter, tells us that true faith produces works, and he gives us two examples—first Abraham and then Rahab. He gives them as parallels. Of Abraham he says, "Was not Abraham our father justified by works, when he offered up Isaac his son on the altar?" (2:21). Of Rahab he says, "And in the same way was not Rahab the harlot also justified by works, when she received the messengers and sent them out by another way?" (2:25). James's point in these two examples is that Abraham showed his faith at great cost. He was willing to offer up his son. Rahab had the same faith; she risked everything. Faith is not a barren, intellectual process. Real, true faith produces action! Have we ever risked anything for our faith? Are we willing to do so, if called to? Is our faith real?

Faith's Formation

We wonder at such great faith, and we wonder where Rahab got it. Abraham Kuyper, a great Biblical scholar who also served as Prime Minister of the Netherlands from 1901-1905, says:

> The people who in Rahab's time most frequently used such houses of prostitution were the traveling merchants. From them she had repeatedly heard of the marvelous nation which was approaching from Egypt, and of the God of Israel who had perfected such striking miracles.[7]

Rahab heard that there was only one God, Jehovah. She heard bits and snatches about Israel's destiny. She heard, perhaps derisively, of the nation's high ethical and moral code. Perhaps (and this is only a conjecture) she had become disillusioned with the culture around her. She was treated as chattel. She had seen life at its worst. All of this together made her open to truth and faith.

No doubt fear contributed to the formation of her faith. Fear is an inevitable and natural consequence of sensing that God's justice leaves us in the wrong. Rahab knew she was a sinner. She was ready for faith.

Then there was the testimony of the spies, which opened her to faith. Rahab must immediately have sensed the difference between the Israelite visitors and those who normally frequented her house. They were not sensualists, but men of high morals. She had never seen this before. They were sure of their God. Their ethos confirmed the reality of what she had been hearing from the merchants. This, along with her disillusionment and fear, coalesced to produce her faith. Rahab's speech in verses 9-11 is a song of belief in the one God:

> I know that the Lord has given you the land, and that the terror of you has fallen on us, and that all the inhabitants of the land have melted away before you. For we have heard how the Lord dried up the water of the Red Sea before you when you came out of Egypt, and what you did to the two kings of the Amorites who were beyond the Jordan, to Sihon and Og, whom you utterly destroyed. And when we heard it, our hearts melted and no courage remained in any man any longer because of you; for the Lord your God, He is God in heaven above and on earth beneath.

Jericho had stood for hundreds of years. Today it is still the earliest fortified town known to scholarship.[8] Its inhabitants thought it invincible. But Rahab heard God's word, and though she was surrounded by her ancient culture, which appeared to be eternal, she believed! That is why her faith has been immortalized. Hebrews 11:31 says, "By faith Rahab the harlot did not perish along with those who were disobedient."

We can never tell where faith will be found. There was hope for Rahab, and there is hope for people where we would never dream of it. I would not say this about Charles Colson, except that he said it about himself. Before he came to Christ, as an ambitious, high-powered politician he would have done almost anything to advance his political beliefs. He well deserved the epithet "henchman." But since coming to Christ he has become the incarnation of the Savior to thousands of prisoners in our jails. He has become the hands, eyes, mouth, and feet of Christ to the castoffs of society. There could hardly be a more unlikely candidate for such a transformation. Matthew 8:11 says:

> And I say to you, that many shall come from east and west, and recline at table with Abraham, and Isaac, and Jacob, in the kingdom of heaven.

But the hope is just not out there for others. Rahab's story tells us that there is hope for us with our incomplete, incipient, imperfect, stumbling, selfish faith. God blesses imperfect faith! This great truth ought to cause us to shout for joy!

Faith's Reward

Rahab's faith garnered three rewards. First, Israel was encouraged.

> Then the two men returned and came down from the hill country and crossed over and came to Joshua the son of Nun, and they related to him all that had happened to them. And they said to Joshua, "Surely the Lord has given all the land into our hands, and all the inhabitants of the land, moreover, have melted away before us" (2:23, 24).

The children of Israel were encouraged through Rahab's great confession of faith (vv. 8-11). They were uplifted by the positive report that the spies brought back; and they were strengthened by the miraculous deliverance given to the two spies through the prostitute.

The second reward of Rahab's faith was her own salvation. This came initially as physical salvation, as chapter 6:22-25 records:

> And Joshua said to the two men who had spied out the land, "Go into the harlot's house and bring the woman and all she has out of there as you have sworn to her." So the young men who were spies went in and brought out Rahab and her father and her mother and her brothers and all she had; they also brought out all her relatives, and placed them outside the camp of Israel. And they burned the city with fire, and all that was in it. Only the silver and gold and articles of bronze and iron, they put into the treasure of the house of the Lord. However, Rahab the harlot and her father's household and all she had, Joshua spared; and she has lived in the midst of Israel to this day, for she hid the messengers whom Joshua sent to spy out Jericho.

Rahab did not initially have saving faith in the spiritual sense, but as she joined with Israel she believed completely and became a full member of God's covenant people. Ultimately, Rahab's faith saved her in every way.

The third reward of Rahab's faith may be spoken of as her "glorification." Here her story becomes lyrical. Not only did Rahab live in Israel the rest of her life, but she married an

Israelite and became an ancestor of Jesus Christ. Matthew's genealogy of Jesus tells us:

> . . . and to Ram was born Amminadab; and to Amminadab, Nahshon; and to Nahshon, Salmon; and to Salmon was born Boaz by Rahab; and to Boaz was born Obed by Ruth; and to Obed, Jesse; and to Jesse was born David the King.

And from David's lineage Christ came. Nahshon, Rahab's father-in-law, was one of the twelve princes who made a special offering at the raising of the Tabernacle. Numbers 7:12 says, "Now the one who presented his offering on the first day was Nahshon . . . of the tribe of Judah." Nahshon was a great prince of Judah, and so was his son Salmon who married Rahab. How beautiful—the Amorite prostitute became a believer and then the wife of a prince of Judah. Rahab was a princess and ancestor of Christ!

Amazingly, but predictably, some have been uncomfortable with Rahab's being a princess and an ancestress of Christ. Josephus tried to make her out to be an "innkeeper" (*Ant.* V. 1:2, 7), and some have referred to her as a "landlady" or "formerly a fallen woman." As we have seen, she was a *pornee* and nothing else. I think it is wonderful that she belongs to Christ's bloodline. In fact it fits perfectly! The whole human race is guilty of spiritual prostitution—and all of us have had our lapses. Jesus did not come from a sinless human line. Everyone in it was a sinner in need of salvation, including the Virgin Mary!

Anyone who looks down on Rahab had better beware, for it is obvious that such a person has a defective doctrine of sin and does not understand the depth of human sin or the grace of God. All of us stand in Rahab's place in front of a holy God. And many of us are worse, because she had such little knowledge. We must at least be as wise as Rahab, who, though she understood little, understood that she was under God's judgment and sought redemption.

Hebrews 11:33 tells us Rahab was saved by faith. James 2:25 says it was by works. There is no contradiction—Rahab was saved by a faith that produced works. Her faith, so beautifully symbolized by the scarlet cord, brought her into the mercy of God. What is the sign in your window?

Let us be men and women of faith. Let us be those who see the unseen, who see the promises from afar, who leave Egypt because we see Him. Let us have a faith that works in the midst of a sometimes hostile world.

Footnotes

1. John J. Davis, *Conquest and Crisis, Studies in Joshua, Judges and Ruth* (Grand Rapids: Baker, 1976), n.p.
2. Norman L. Geisler, *The Christian Love Ethic* (Grand Rapids: Zondervan, 1979), pp. 78-80.
3. John Calvin, *Commentaries on the Book of Joshua* (Grand Rapids: Baker, 1984), p. 47.
4. W. Robertson Nicoll, *The Expositor's Bible* (A. C. Armstrong and Son, 1903), p. 89.
5. Martin H. Woudstra, *The Book of Joshua* (Grand Rapids: Eerdmans, 1983), p. 75.
6. Francis A. Schaeffer, *Joshua and the Flow of Biblical History* (Downers Grove, Ill.: InterVarsity Press, 1975), p. 78.
7. Abraham Kuyper, *Women of the Old Testament* (Grand Rapids: Zondervan, 1961), p. 69.
8. Trent C. Butler, *Word Biblical Commentary: Joshua* (Waco, Tex.: Word, 1983), p. 32.

4

CROSSING THE JORDAN
Joshua 3:1-17

The two returned spies, delivered from Jericho through Rahab, ended their report to Joshua with a heartening burst of optimistic confidence.

> Surely the Lord has given all the land into our hands, and all the inhabitants of the land, moreover, have melted away before us (2:24).

That was what Joshua had been waiting for. Immediately he dispatched runners throughout the vast camp, announcing that first thing the next morning they would break camp and pitch their tents on the banks of the Jordan. Verse 1 of chapter 3 records the event:

> Then Joshua rose early in the morning; and he and all the sons of Israel set out from Shittim and came to the Jordan, and they lodged there before they crossed.

The journey from the acacias of Shittim to the banks of the Jordan is an easy one—just a few miles over smooth ground. We can therefore assume that the Israelites probably finished their march well before the sun had risen high in the sky.

The Jordan River channel consisted of the regular riverbed; the Zor, a surrounding level of desolate gray soil unfit for habitation or cultivation because constant flooding eroded the topsoil; and then the Ghor, which was fertile and green. Israel encamped on the Ghor, close to the river's edge, which now covered the middle area because it was flood time (3:15). Israel's multiple hundreds of thousands must have presented an unforgettable sight as they camped in the traditional orderliness, tribe by tribe, along the raging Jordan.

There they remained three days, watching the torrent race by, and looking across to long-awaited Canaan. The waiting was meant to impress them with the seeming impossibility of the task. Perhaps a few could swim the Jordan, but there was no way they could manage this with the babies and the infirm and aged, not to mention their possessions. We can be sure that many a passionate doubt was muttered across their night fires. Some doubted Joshua had the "right stuff." Leading them here in flood season was an obvious mistake. Moses would never have been so foolish.

But the Lord had a plan which they knew nothing about, and the text of chapter 3 records how God revealed the steps they must take to cross the impossible Jordan—and the success that was theirs in following His advice. This chapter was to become a key passage in Israel's self-understanding, for it taught them the greatness of God and what He required of His people who would move forward with Him. It can also be the key to a similar self-understanding for us, for it describes *three steps* required to ford the seemingly impossible difficulties which confront us, and to take further possession of our own spiritual inheritance.

First, Israel Was to Follow the Ark of the Covenant (vv. 2-4)

Verses 2 and 3 record the command:

> And it came about at the end of three days that the officers went through the midst of the camp; and they commanded the people, saying, "When you see the ark of the covenant of the Lord your God with the Levitical priests carrying it, then you shall set out from your place and go after it."

Obviously, there was deep significance in this command to follow the Ark. The question we must ask is, What did it mean to the Israelites? Primarily, it meant following God's presence. The Ark was a simple box four feet long, two and a half feet high, and two and a half feet wide. It contained the tablets of stone upon which the finger of God had written the Ten Commandments. It also held a pot of manna—which witnessed to God's gracious provision during the preceding forty years (cf. Exodus 16:33, 34). The Ark was topped with a gold plate called the Mercy Seat over which two statues of cherubim knelt (cf. Exodus 25:18, 19). Psalm 80:1 and 99:1 describe God as "enthroned above the cherubim." Everything about the Ark exuded the presence of God.

Not only did the Ark symbolize the presence of God, but He was indeed specially present in and with it. The Philistines found this out in a way never to be forgotten when they captured the Ark and brought it into the house of Dagon, their god. The two nights the Ark spent in Dagon's house resulted in Dagon's falling before the Ark, fully dismembered. Not only did Dagon suffer grave indignities, but the people themselves were smitten with tumors (very likely bubonic plague) so that they implored the Israelites to take it back (1 Samuel 5:1-18). God was in the Ark! God's presence would go before them over the Jordan and into the land. God would, so to speak, take the first steps into Canaan. Their duty was to follow God's presence.

Verse 4 lays out the procedure very clearly:

> However, there shall be between you and it a distance of about two thousand cubits by measure. Do not come near it, that you may know the way by which you shall go, for you have not passed this way before.

Two thousand cubits is equivalent to one kilometer or about six-tenths of a mile, a Sabbath's day journey. Why the specific distance? The text tells us that it was so all of Israel could have a good view of the Ark and thus of God's direction. Had they crowded in close, only a handful would have seen it. Picture the scene. All Israel is encamped on the sloping Ghor and the Ark is positioned two thousand cubits from them. Everyone in the nation can see it. All eyes are commanded to be fixed upon it. God was telling Israel that the Jordan would be breached and victory would come as they *focused* on and *followed* God. This was to be basic to Israel's self-understanding.

What this means to us is clear enough with one sublime addition: Jesus Christ, when He walked on this earth, was the true Ark of God! The Ark was the physical abode of the Divine Presence, and Christ is the reality of the Divine Presence with men. He was Emmanuel, "God with us" (Matthew 1:23). Everything in the Ark pointed to Christ, who fulfilled the Law (Matthew 5:17) and was the manna, the bread of God (John 6:31-46). Jesus became the Mercy Seat for us,

> whom God displayed publicly as a propitiation in His blood through faith (Romans 3:25).
>
> . . . and He Himself is the propitiation for our sins; and not ours only, but also for those of the whole world (1 John 2:2).

He is the obedient One who kept God's Law perfectly. He is the merciful One who makes it possible for a holy God to show mercy to sinful men.

We must focus on and follow Jesus, the living Ark of God, who was and is God of God, Light of Light, Very God of Very God, if we are to ford our Jordans and more fully enjoy His spiritual riches. This is what we read in Hebrews 12:2: "fixing our eyes upon Jesus, the author and perfecter of faith." This is basic for the whole Christian life.

This is what Peter's experience with God in walking on the water was all about. Fixing his eyes on the Master as He shouted "Come!" Peter began to ply the seas. But when he took his eyes off Jesus and saw the raging elements, he began to sink (Matthew 14:27-31). We are to *focus* and *follow*. We must be like the Psalmist who could say, "My eyes are continually toward the Lord" (Psalm 25:15). Are there any rivers you think are uncrossable? Is there something in life which is keeping you from the richness God wants for you? If so, fix your eyes upon Jesus!

Second, Israel Was to Sanctify Themselves (v. 5)

The second step God gave Israel for bridging life's difficulties was to sanctify themselves. In verse 5 we read, "Then Joshua said to the people, 'Consecrate (sanctify) yourselves, for tomorrow the Lord will do wonders among you.'" God was telling Israel that a holy life is the natural and proper personal equipment for those who wish to be borne across the difficulties blocking their advancement.

One of the prime reasons ancient Israel found the way blocked, as do Christians today, is sin. Isaiah wrote:

> Behold, the Lord's hand is not so short that it cannot save; neither is His ear so dull that it cannot hear. But your iniquities have made a separation between you and your God, and your sins hide His face from you, so that He does not hear (59:1, 2).

How true to our spiritual experience this is. Later, in the land, the sin of one man, Achan, brought misery on the entire nation. His sin shortened the Lord's arm and turned His face away—and many of his kinsmen died in what should have been an easy victory (Joshua 7).

Here, on the eve of one of the great days in their history, when they would miraculously cross into the Promised Land, the people of Israel sanctified themselves. Perhaps there was some external ceremonial washing, but whatever they did was essentially internal and spiritual. God's people examined their lives, purged known sins, resolved to forsake them, and consecrated themselves to God's service.

The applications of this truth are many, but perhaps a personal word will serve best. My experience has been that when I face a hurdle which obviously requires God's power to surmount, it is imperative that I examine my heart, confess all known sin, and then recommit myself to Him. I do not do this legalistically, thinking that now I will merit God's power. But I do it with an eye to removing those obstacles to my being used. I have found this absolutely necessary wherever my Jordan lies, whether in my family relationships, personal business, church business, or preaching.

God's power courses freely over those who sanctify themselves for Him. Like God's children on the bank of the Jordan, we need to do two things: 1) fix our unwavering gaze on Jesus, and 2) set ourselves apart for His service. Only then can God work fully through us.

Third, Israel Was to Step Out and Stand Still (vv. 7-13)

If you have done this, there remains one more thing; that is to step out and stand still. God first informed Joshua of this as we read in verses 7, 8:

> Now the Lord said to Joshua, "This day I will begin to exalt you in the sight of all Israel, that they may know that just as I have been with Moses, I will be with you. You shall, moreover, command the priests who are carrying the ark of the covenant, saying, 'When you come to the edge of the waters of the Jordan, you shall stand still in the Jordan.'"

Joshua, in turn, relays this truth to his people in verse 13, adding that the result will be that the Jordan will dry up.

> And it shall come about when the soles of the feet of the priests who carry the ark of the Lord, the Lord of all the earth, shall rest in the waters of the Jordan, the waters of the Jordan shall be cut off, and the waters which are flowing down from above shall stand in one heap.

The point here is that nothing would happen as long as they stood still. The vanguard of Israel (representing all their people) had to step out into the water in faith. This is one of the great truths of life: nothing will happen unless we are, by faith, willing to get our feet wet. Focusing on the Ark, focusing on Jesus, is good. Sanctifying ourselves is also good. Both are essential. But little will come of these things unless we take the initial step of faith. Our eyes and our hearts can be right on, but if we do not move out to meet the challenges, we will never progress in God's work. If we are ever going to do anything for God, we must clearly be willing to take the kind of steps that get our feet wet.

But it is also true that if we are ever going to accomplish anything for God, we must be willing to stand still just as the vanguard of Israel did—as they awaited the power of God. In all their activity of faith, they maintained a brilliant passivity. Their standing still testified to the fact that everything came from God. They were acting, but all their human activity would come to nothing if God did not show His power.

How beautiful their faith was as we see it in their stepping out and their standing. None of us will get across our Jordans if with our step of faith we do not also stand in faith.

Crossing the Jordan

Picture the scene. The fabled Jordan had risen far above its banks. Myriads and myriads of Israelites stretched along her banks and far back up on the plain. There stood the armed warriors with sword and shield, the aged men trembling on their staffs, wide-eyed mothers and helpless infants of only a day. There also the flocks brought from Egypt milled about, and the people's possessions lay in heaps. In the river stood the Ark on the shoulders of the priests. The space around was clear for two thousand cubits. All Israel had their eyes on the Ark. All Israel had been sanctified. The vanguard had taken the steps of faith. Now they were standing in faith. A great hush fell upon the people.

Then they saw the river level was dropping fast! Somewhere up the river (at the city of Adam some nineteen miles to the north, to be exact) the waters mounted up in a great crystal heap. The riverbed was dry. In fact, it was bare all the way south to the Dead Sea! Now a rolling, thunderous roar went up from Israel and the people began to cross rapidly, without confusion, in a great swath which extended for a mile or more.

This stupendous event became one of the milestones in Israel's self-understanding. The manner of their entering the Promised Land was indelibly printed upon Israel's consciousness. In future years they sang of it, as the words of Psalm 114:3-6 reveal:

> The sea looked and fled;
> The Jordan turned back.
> The mountains skipped like rams,
> The hills like lambs.
> What ails you, O sea, that you flee?
> O Jordan, that you turn back?
> O mountains, that you skip like rams?
> O hills, like lambs?

They were again reminded, as they entered the Promised Land, that God can do anything. They were light-years beyond the modern theology of Harold Kushner, who no longer believes God is all-powerful. Jeremiah shouted:

> Ah, Lord God! Behold, Thou hast made the heavens and the earth by Thy great power and by Thine outstretched arm! Nothing is too difficult for Thee (32:17).

Job confidently asserted at the end of his experience: "I know that Thou canst do all things and no purpose of Thee can be thwarted" (Job 42:2). The people were reassured that God's protection went with them as they followed Him.

> When you pass through the waters, I will be with you; and through the rivers, they will not overflow you. When you walk through the fire, you will not be scorched, nor will the flame burn you (Isaiah 43:2).

A Blessed Awareness

Lastly, the steps of this crossing were branded on their corporate consciousness. When facing future Jordans, they now knew, they must focus their eyes upon God, sanctify themselves for Him, step out in faith, and stand in faith.

This great story is also a key for our self-understanding. He has Jordans He wants us to cross; beyond them lies land which He wants us to occupy, where our service will be enhanced and life will be richer. Israel's experience teaches us that we must believe He can do anything. We must hold this truth dearly. We must never surrender to the naturalism and pessimism which grips so much Christianity. God can do anything He desires.

We must focus on Christ, our Ark, who fulfilled the Law, was manna, bread from heaven, and became our Mercy Seat by supplying His own blood. We must cast out all sin, and set ourselves apart as sanctified for the holy tasks He has for us.

When He commands us, we must step out in faith with *blessed activity,* but then we must also stand motionless in *blessed passivity*—for it is God who does it, who is our all, in all, under all, wholly above presiding, wholly below sustaining. Do you have any Jordans you think are impossible? Any rivers you think are uncrossable? If God is leading you to cross them, you can and you will.

5

"WHAT DO THESE STONES MEAN?" Joshua 4:1-24

The nation of Israel now spread across the great Jordan River. Far to the north, some nineteen miles away, near the city of Adam (3:16), the waters were stopped in one great swelling heap, leaving a barren riverbed all the way south to the Dead Sea. At the point of Israel's crossing stood the Ark of the Covenant, high on the shoulders of priests in the center of the dry channel, as thousands upon thousands passed by, carefully keeping the prescribed two thousand cubits distance. Beyond the barren swath about the Ark as far as one could see, looking north and south, moved God's people with babes in arms, driving their flocks, pushing their carts. Though the people moved quickly, it was hours until the rear guard appeared, as the tribes of Reuben and Gad and the half-tribe of Manasseh crossed over with their forty thousand warriors in full battle array.

The motionless Ark and the flowing sea of humanity made a remarkable contrast. The Ark watched over all in silent repose. Vast as the miracle was, the great demonstration of power was nothing for God. Infinite power went out, but the power remained constant, suffering no depletion. Israel's self-awareness was to be saturated with the understanding that their God could do anything for them—and that whatever He did He did with the ease of omnipotence.

Now all the Israelites, except Joshua and twelve select men (one from each tribe), stood on the west bank of the Jordan. They had entered the Promised Land—and their presence dominated the horizon. Then God spoke to Joshua, as the opening verses of chapter 4 record beginning with verse 2:

> Take for yourselves twelve men from the people, one man from each tribe, and command them, saying, "Take up for yourselves twelve stones from here out of the middle of the Jordan, from the place where the priests' feet are standing firm, and carry them over with you, and lay them down in the lodging place where you will lodge tonight." So Joshua called the twelve men whom he had appointed from the sons of Israel, one man from each tribe; and Joshua said to them, "Cross again to the Ark of the Lord your God into the middle of the Jordan, and each of you take up a stone on his shoulder, according to the number of the tribes of the sons of Israel."

Israel Builds Memorials

As Israel stood gazing on, the twelve select men solemnly descended the banks and approached the Ark. Then, kneeling at the priests' feet, each pried a large stone from the river bottom and began a reverent procession up the west bank and across the plain to Gilgal. To the symbol-oriented Israelites, the significance of the twelve stones was easily understood. They represented the twelve tribes of Israel and their deliverance from the river. Arriving in Gilgal, the twelve men stacked the rocks into a small mound—a very unimpressive one, especially in reference to the momentous event which they commemorated. Having completed this, the twelve then each selected a stone from dry land and walked back to the Ark, where they formed a duplicate mound on the riverbed.

It was fitting that they commemorate the place where the Ark of their covenant God delivered them. Poetically, it served as a seal to Israel's possession of the Promised Land. If any Israelite decided to flee back into the wilderness, there would be the stones of deliverance crying out against him.

Then, for the first time in hours, the Ark began to move, as the weary priests who bore it slowly moved up the bank toward the Ghor. When the last priest's foot crossed the edge, back roared the fabled Jordan, and a tumultuous cheer rolled across the great host of Israel.

A Place to Remember

The celebration in Gilgal (which means "the reproach has been rolled away") must have been something to behold; the people rejoiced that the reproach of forty years of wandering was over. We can be sure that most of them danced and sang around their fires far into the night. The word *Hebrew* means "people from across the river." The name now became a prophecy fulfilled. They had been waiting centuries, since the time of Abraham, for this day. Perhaps Joshua himself joined the dancing around the campfires. Perhaps he was too tired, but we can be sure of this—he returned to observe in the flickering light that mound of crude, unworked stones from the bottom of the Jordan. God had done it! Again and again he reran the mental "tapes" of that day through his mind. God was with him! God's power could do anything! His leadership was verified! He was God's man! Verse 19 tells us that the calendar date was "the tenth of the first month"—the day (the very day!) forty years before that the first Passover Lamb was selected (Exodus 12:6), which led to their crossing the Red Sea.

The Puritan Matthew Henry says of this:

> God so ordered it so that they should enter Canaan four days before the annual solemnity of the Passover, and on the very day when the preparation for it was to begin . . . because he would have their entrance into Canaan graced and sanctified with that religious feast, and would have them to be reminded of their deliverance out of Egypt, that, comparing them together, God might be glorified as the *Alpha* and *Omega* of their bliss.[1]

Joshua had much to think about as he viewed those stones, and he thought a lot about them over the years. Gilgal became the command headquarters for conquering the Promised Land. It was the place to which he frequently returned after victories, in the midst of battles, and after his defeats such as that of Ai. Here he gathered wisdom and strength to go on, for here lay the stones of remembrance.

The Purpose of the Memorials

The overall purpose of those two piles of stones was to bring God's people to reflect on what happened on that great event, as verses 6 and 7 record in God's words:

> Let this be a sign among you, so that when your children ask later, saying, "What do these stones mean to you?" then you shall say to them, "Because the waters of the Jordan were cut off before the ark of the covenant of the Lord; when it crossed the Jordan, the waters of the Jordan were cut off." So these stones shall become a memorial to the sons of Israel forever.

Later in the chapter (vv. 21-23), Joshua says substantively the same thing to the people. Here we must realize that this idea of a "memorial" or remembering in Hebrew is more than a recalling to mind. It involves remembering with concern; it also implies loving reflection and then action.[2] The Israelites were to look on the stones of remembrance and realize that they did not get across the Jordan on their own ability, but that everything was of God. And, realizing this, they were to conduct all of life accordingly, whether it be family life, business, or warfare.

Behind the general purpose of changing the way Israel was to approach life lay an ultimate and higher purpose—that of fearing God. Joshua explains this purpose in the final verse of our chapter, verse 24:

> . . . that all the peoples of the earth may know that the hand of the Lord is mighty, so that you may fear the Lord your God forever.

Through these stones, God wanted to promote fear among His people. That does not mean He intended them to dread Him; rather, He wished to inspire something quite beautiful, for fear carries the idea that the people recognize God's glory and majesty and then submit to Him in trust. The contemplation of the stones would do something wonderful for them, eventuating loving reverence and trust. The contemplation of the great works of God would elevate their spiritual lives.

What Do These Stones Mean?

Over the years godly Israelites would pass by these stones, perhaps even make family pilgrimages, and their children would ask, "What do these stones mean?" Then their parents would recount in detail the great story, and thus their children would be caught up in reverential awe and begin to relate to God with faith they had not known before. It really did happen, and it can still happen today.

Building memorials (remembering the great things God has done) is of the highest importance. Here it happened because of a direct command of God. This is highly significant. The stones were *not* Joshua's idea, nor that of any other man. God commanded them because He knows how important remembering what He has done is for spiritual health. This is the reason He instituted the Passover feast as a remembrance. In Exodus 12:26, 27 He commanded Israel saying:

> And it will come about when your children will say to you, "What does this rite mean to you?" that you shall say, "It is a Passover sacrifice to the Lord who passed over the houses of the sons of Israel in Egypt when He smote the Egyptians, but spared our homes."

He commanded much the same thing regarding the Law in Deuteronomy 6:20-23:

> When your son asks you in time to come, saying, "What do the testimonies and the statutes and the judgments mean which the Lord commanded you?" then you shall say to your son, "We were slaves to Pharaoh in Egypt; and the Lord brought us from Egypt with a mighty hand. Moreover, the Lord showed great and distressing signs and wonders before our eyes against Egypt, Pharaoh and all his household; and He brought us out from there in order to bring us in, to give us the land which He had sworn to our fathers."

Why this stress on remembering? Because God's people have always seemed to forget the great things He has done. The seventy-two verses of Psalm 78 mournfully chronicle Israel's tendency to forget God despite His faithfulness. Verses 10 and 11 say it all:

> They did not keep the covenant of God,
> And refused to walk in His Law;
> And they forgot His deeds,
> And His miracles that He had shown them.
> (Cf. Psalm 106:13.)

All of us must attempt to remember what God has done for us personally and for others of His children past and present. Such remembering does wonders for our souls. Isaiah 51:9, 10 describes Isaiah's reflections on the great things God did in the past, and then verse 11 records his hymn of faith:

> So the ransomed of the Lord will return, and come with joyful shouting to Zion; and everlasting joy will be on their heads. They will obtain gladness and joy, and sorrow and sighing will flee away.

That is what remembering does! Peter, in 2 Peter 2:5–8, remembers how God preserved Noah and delivered Lot, then concludes with this resounding statement of confidence in verse 9:

> . . . then the Lord knows how to rescue the godly from temptation, and to keep the unrighteous under punishment for the day of judgment.

If He did it for them, He can do it for us! Psalm 119:52 says, "I have remembered Thine ordinances from of old, O Lord, and comfort myself." It is imperative that we build memorials, make conscious attempts to preserve the memory of the great things God has done for us.

Building Memorials in Our Lives

Remembering God's work in our lives can act as a tonic for us all. Let me share some stones of remembrance from my own family's experience.

The first goes back more than ten years to the time when I had accepted the call to begin a new church. I remember well the day after my call, taking my wife, Barbara, and driving out to the city of Brea, California, where the church was to be, and looking for the best piece of land—and I found it. It was four acres situated in the middle of a beautiful residential district, two blocks from the freeway where there was a mall development; twelve minutes to the south was Disneyland; ten minutes away was Angel Stadium. It was like heaven on earth! I remember asking that God might give us that property.

I found out that the local Presbyterian Synod had bought it nineteen years earlier. When I called they said, "People have been trying to buy that property for years, but we did not want to sell. Two weeks ago we made the decision to sell and you are the first one to call." I remember sitting down at a nice restaurant with some representatives of the Synod, who said, "We don't really want to sell the property." Running through my mind was the thought it would be a lot of money. As we began to talk, I found that one of those men, years before, had served as Sunday school superintendent at the church where my father's sister-in-law had served. He softened up and said to me, "We paid $150,000 nineteen years ago and have paid $5,000 in taxes. I want you to have that property. If you'll give us $155,000, you can have it." We had 180-day escrow, raised the money, and paid cash.

Some tough times were ahead in giving birth to that church, but I always had the miracle of the property to look back to and say, "What do the stones and dirt clods of this remarkable property mean?" They meant God is a God of miracles. They meant He can do anything He pleases. They meant He loves me and cares about my ministry. They meant that I can believe Him. And they mean the same thing today to me and my family.

Another stone of remembrance for my family came at Christmas many years ago when my pet-loving children were small. We were pastoring a small church and things were tight. The situation worsened when our English bulldog, Precious, had to have an operation—and everything hit the bottom when we all returned one night to find our tomcat, Prudence, near death due to a run-in with a car or a baseball bat. To live, Prudence would have to have an operation which would take all the money we had saved for our children's presents. We put it to the children: it was the operation and no Christmas presents, or presents and no Prudence. Predictably, they chose Prudence. But they also got a beautiful Christmas—because someone who knew nothing about the situation sent us a check designated for "Christmas presents only." So we had our bandaged Prudence and Precious and presents, too! Our children, and their parents, have never forgotten this. What does this memory mean to us? It would take all of us to tell.

Another stone of remembrance is really my son Carey's, and it came when he got himself a "state of the art" motorcross bicycle. It was the envy of all the kids in the neighborhood. He bought it used, but it was really spectacular. Then it was stolen from our front yard. In Southern California that means the handlebars go one way, the wheels go another, and the frame gets repainted. It was gone! But he prayed. A month later, while driving down a busy boulevard, we looked to the side of the road and there was his bicycle, lying abandoned, but in perfect shape. Carey said, "God answered my prayers." That's a stone of remembrance.

A final stone of remembrance has to do with my son Kent and a rainbow. We were on vacation in the Rocky Mountains and had spent the morning fishing, and Kent said he wanted to talk about God and other things. So that afternoon we walked down a ravine, settled in under a pine tree for shelter because it was misting, and began to talk. He had a lot of hard questions which were about the existence of God. It is difficult to believe in a Being you cannot see. He was asking the questions many think, but do not always ask. I was answering the best I could, but not always to his satisfaction. But our talk was long and good. Finally we prayed together and climbed up out of the ravine. I will never forget Kent's words: "Dad, look—two rainbows!" And there were two distinct rainbows, separate from one another, not concentric progressions of the same spectrum. Two rainbows. And, thinking of Noah's rainbow, Kent said, "It's a sign. One for you and one for me!" For him it was an affirmation of God's existence.

All of us have "stones of remembrance," some less concrete, some more; some more dramatic, others less. And God has given them to us to look back on and rejoice, that we might reverence Him and serve Him in devoted faith.

Getting Serious about Remembering

All of us need to pile some stones up as we go through life. It should become a habitual part of our journey. A primary reason for this is that we so easily forget the good and remember the bad. Slights, injuries, disappointments, misfortunes lodge readily in our memories. Benevolences, kindnesses, satisfactions, even miracles slip easily away. Our Christian duty is to remember, because of the danger, as with Israel, of forgetting. We need to gather stones of remembrance because of what they do for us. They build personal confidence and courage. In 2 Corinthians 1:8, 9 Paul remembers how God delivered him from death when he thought it was all over, and then confidently says, God ". . . will deliver us, He in whom we have set our hope. And He will yet deliver us." These Gilgals, these remembrances, benefit everyone! Our spouses are strengthened. Our children grow as they ask, "What do these stones mean?" And the Body of Christ takes on new vitality.

Joshua 4 is a call to remember the miracles and graces of God in our lives, and then to share them with our families and our church. Realizing that God commanded Israel to do so at the Jordan justifies forcefully calling us to do so! The question is, how?

> Set aside some time alone to read Joshua 4 and try to recall times you have experienced the power of God. Few of us will have anything quite as dramatic as the parting of the Jordan in our lives. I only have a few remembrances, like the Lord miraculously providing property for a new church. But all of us have some remarkable memories of special provision or special power which came into our lives—even if for a fleeting moment. List these things.
>
> If you are a part of a family, or perhaps a small fellowship, make a habit of sharing your remembrances around the table. Do it naturally. Don't say, "All right, children, now it is time to share our stones. . . ." Be sensitive and natural. Share authentically. Be honest.
>
> Birthdays are perfect times for parents to reminisce about God's provisions. The holidays also provide

possible times to get Grandma and Grandpa to share. One family in our church has attached a memory to each ornament on the Christmas tree, so that they annually take time to remember God's goodness to them.

Something you might also consider is making a scrapbook to record the Gilgals in your life and giving it a title out of Joshua 4.

A remembering people, a people who, like Joshua of old, would ride back into camp and contemplate those stones from the Jordan, are a people who will fear their God and do great exploits. Let us follow God's Word and "forget none of His benefits."

Footnotes

1. *Matthew Henry's Commentary on the Whole Bible,* Vol. 2 (Old Tappan, N.J.: Revell, n.d.), pp. 2l, 22.
2. M. H. Woudstra, *The Book of Joshua* (Grand Rapids: Eerdmans, 1981), p. 92.

6

THE CAPTAIN OF THE HOST
Joshua 5:13-15

Israel had crossed the Jordan. Virtually nothing remained before the opening shots of the campaign for possession of the land of Canaan. The sight of the twelve stones in the midst of the camp at Gilgal repeatedly triggered Joshua's memories of the last few weeks' incredible events. Again and again he recalled the gleaming Ark above the shoulders of the priests as it moved into the Jordan, and the rolling thunder of his people's voices as the waters began to recede. Looking at the stones of remembrance, he repeatedly pictured his people extending as far as the eye could see to the north and south, joyously crossing the river. Over and over he envisioned the Ark leaving the dry bed, and the Jordan River flooding back and overflowing its borders, as his people watched for miles high up on the west banks. Joshua's heart welled within him, and he was ready to move out for God.

The crossing completed, Joshua took steps to reaffirm his people's covenantal relationship with God; he circumcised all the males born in the wilderness (vv. 2-9) and celebrated the Passover (v. 10). All Israel made a renewed commitment to Jehovah. With this, the supply of manna from heaven ceased for the first time in thirty-eight years, and the people began to feed themselves from the produce of the land. Israel, too, was now ready.

War loomed only hours away. Behind the masses of God's people, the flooding Jordan blocked all retreat. Before them rose the ominous ramparts of Jericho, her gates shut, sealed tight, and her men of war on the walls. Most of the Israelites had never seen a fortified city; knowing the recurrent pessimism of this people, we can be sure that fears ran high in the camp—despite the great things God had done for them.

Humanly speaking, Joshua bore all the lonely responsibility of leadership. He needed to get away to pray, to meditate, to plan the conquest. How he would liked to have Moses there to talk to. But there was no Moses. Joshua had sole authority.

A Divine Encounter

So he stole out of camp in the darkness to view Jericho for himself and seek God's guidance. The Hebrew word which tells us that Joshua was "by Jericho" (verse 14) expresses the idea of immediate proximity.[1] He was very close, perhaps close enough to feel the oppression of the city described as "walled to heaven." There he remained in the night—brooding, meditating, patrolling, his eyes fixed to the ground—when he detected some movement on the periphery of his vision and raised his eyes. What he saw set his heart racing and adrenalin pumping. For there stood a warrior in full battle dress, his sword bare and gleaming blue in the moon's light. A less courageous man would have bolted. But not Joshua. His hand no doubt upon his own sword, he strode forward, calling out to the figure, "Are you for us or for our adversaries?" (verse 13). "Which side are you on—ours or the enemy's? Because if you are from Jericho, then it will be steel against steel!" Joshua was no armchair general.

There was no way Joshua could anticipate the sublimity ahead. He could not possibly know that the next few minutes would become a spiritual bench mark in his life. This mystic encounter was Joshua's final personal spiritual preparation for the challenge of conquest. Afterwards, he would go forth with even stronger courage and boldness. For Joshua it was a greater moment than the crossing of the Jordan.

Our situation, of course, is far less dramatic than his, and our responsibilities less; yet Joshua's experience shows us what is spiritually necessary to meet the challenge of life successfully.

The First Necessity: A Revelation of the Lord (vv. 13, 14a)

Joshua's ringing challenge was met by an answer that put him flat on his face.

> "No, rather I indeed come now as captain of the host of the Lord." And Joshua fell on his face to the earth, and bowed down, and said to him, "What has my lord to say to his servant?" (v. 14).

I believe (along with Calvin, Keil and Delitzsch, and Maclaren) that this "captain of the host of the Lord" was a theophany, an appearance of Jehovah in the form of an angel or messenger. I believe this for several reasons. First, Joshua was told to take off his shoes, and this very same command was given to Moses *by God* from the burning bush. Exodus 3:5, 6 reads:

> Then He said, "Do not come near here; remove your sandals from your feet, for the place on which you are standing is holy ground." He said also, "I am the God of your father, the God of Abraham, the God of Isaac, and the God of Jacob." Then Moses hid his face, for he was afraid to look at God.

Joshua is to realize, through this command, that the One who speaks is the same God who spoke to Moses. Second, the "captain of the host" who speaks to Joshua is identified as the Lord in the instructions He gives in 6:2-5, introduced by "And *the Lord* said to Joshua . . ." Third, as Origen said in his Sixth Homily on Joshua, "Joshua knew not only that he was of God, but that he was God. For he would not have worshipped him, had he not recognized him to be God."[2] These three points convince me that the "captain of the host" was God in angelic form—"the angel of the Lord."

This appearance was meant to steel Joshua for what lay ahead. We know that it did so from the chapters that follow and from similar events in the lives of other Biblical models. Moses had tried to be a leader, but was impotent until he met the angel of the Lord, when God appeared to him in the burning bush (Exodus 3:2-6). After that he became a fountain of spiritual power. A profound sense of God's presence revolutionized his life. Moses' understanding was again enhanced when he besought God for a further revelation of Himself, saying, "I pray Thee, show me Thy glory!" (Exodus 33:18). The Lord's response—hiding Moses in the cleft of the rock and covering him with His hand while His glory passed by (Exodus 33:20-24)—further strengthened Moses for his unparalleled leadership. His unique awareness of God set him apart from the rest of Israel.

The same is memorably true of Paul. It began with the Lord's appearance to him on the Damascus road (Acts 9:3-16). To be sure, it was less revealing than what Moses and Joshua saw, but it was real. Later, however, Paul had an experience equal to that of Moses. Second Corinthians 12:2-4 describes it:

> I know a man in Christ who fourteen years ago—whether in the body I do not know, or out of the body I do not know, God knows—such a man was caught up to the third heaven. And I know how such a man—whether in the body or apart from the body I do not know, God knows—was caught up into Paradise, and heard inexpressible words, which a man is not permitted to speak.

This experience made Paul the invincible brick he remained throughout the incessant persecutions of his life. Paul did not waver, thanks to the revelation he had of God and his resulting sense of God's presence. I believe that this deep awareness is what set him above the rest of his fellow apostles. God was real. He was present. Paul believed it with all his being.

This awareness makes all the difference in our lives. It is a primary work of the Holy Spirit, which Jesus describes in John 14:16, 17 where Jesus says that He will send another Comforter (the word is *allos,* which means "another of the same kind"). He will send, through the Holy Spirit, a Comforter who will be just like Him. Thus, through the work of the Spirit, you and I sense the presence of God. One of the great ministries of the Holy Spirit is to bring this divine reality to our lives, to make it so real that it is virtually palpable.

It should affect our vision, our imagination, so that we see the presence of God. The first chapter of Revelation tells us that He walks among the churches. He walks down the aisles of our own churches today; He stands on the platform before His assembled people. As Augustine said, "Where Christ, there the church."

We all will face difficulties, but if we have a transcending sense of His presence, we will be steeled for those difficulties and emerge victorious. How sanctifying, how edifying, how upbuilding is the sense of the presence of God! He is more fully real than anything we can see with our natural eyes, for our eyes look only on the temporal, but He is eternal and the unseen things are eternal (2 Corinthians 3:18).

Charles Spurgeon wrote:

> I desire . . . that you exercise your minds, your faith, your spiritual powers and vividly believe that Jesus is here; so believe it, so that your inner eye beholds what you believe.[3]

Because this is so necessary, part of my own devotional regimen is first devoted to focusing on the presence of God. If we have that reality now, then regardless of the Jerichos that come our way, we will triumph. Pray for it, seek it, make it a part of your life. Ask the Holy Spirit. It is His job to give it to you.

The Second Necessity: A Realization that the Lord Will Fight for Us (v. 14)

The walled city of the enemy, the mystic presence of the angel of the Lord in the dark, his sword wrung from the scabbard and held ready—these were permanently impressed on Joshua's consciousness. This vision remained always before him. That raised sword meant that God was going along to fight for Joshua and Israel. It meant that though Israel could mobilize thousands, its forces would be matched and exceeded by a heavenly mobilization.

Elisha knew this and experienced it. He had spoiled the plans of the Syrians by telling the King of Israel what they intended to do, and the King of Syria had found out. When Elisha's servant went out in the morning he saw a huge army around them, ready to take them both. Terrified, he came running to Elisha, who said,

> "Do not fear, for those who are with us are more than those who are with them." Then Elisha prayed and said, "O Lord, I pray, open his eyes, that he may see." And the Lord opened the servant's eyes, and he saw; and behold, the mountain was full of horses and chariots of fire all around Elisha (2 Kings 6:16, 17).

> So to faith's enlightened sight
> All the mountains flamed in the light.

General Joshua himself came to view life this way. When his people saw the impassable walls

> he with enlightened sight,
> saw them ringed with light.

Oh, that we would see life like this. If we have battles to fight, He stands with us, His sword bare and His hosts encircling our enemies. This is not just poetry. Dick Farstadt, who served with HCJB, gave me a transcript of a conversation with a Quechua Indian pastor named Camilo who ministers high in the Andes. In it Camilo tells how a certain radical segment of the townspeople had plotted to beat and kill him and his family, but nothing had come of it. Later they learned why. The transcript of Camilo's words reads as follows:

> One day our neighbors asked my wife, "Is it true that you take soldiers to your house every night to guard you? That's what they say. The other afternoon when people from the cooperative went to your house, they saw many soldiers going back and forth by your doorway. When they saw that, they were really frightened, so much so that they don't remember their return (escape). Filled with fear they scattered in every direction."
>
> We told them that we had not taken even one soldier to our house. . . . We thought, "God probably sent His angels." Then we gave thanks to God.

What do we learn from this? Just this: "If God is for us, who is against us?" (Romans 8:31). We also learn that we do not fight with conventional weapons.

> For though we walk in the flesh, we do not war according to the flesh, for the weapons of our warfare are not of the flesh, but divinely powerful for the destruction of fortresses (2 Corinthians 10:3, 4).

The Third Necessity: Submissive Worship to the Lord (vv. 14b, 15)

The moonlight revealed Joshua doing three things before the Lord:

> And Joshua fell on his face to the earth, and bowed down, and said to him, "What has my lord to say to his servant?" And the captain of the Lord's host said to Joshua, "Remove your sandals from your feet, for the place where you are standing is holy." And Joshua did so.

First, he hit the sand immediately with no hesitation—instant submission. Next, he verbalized his commitment: "What has my lord to say to his servant?" "Lord, You say it, I'll do it!" Third, he responded immediately to the command to remove his sandals in holy reverence. Remember, this is General Joshua, Field Marshal Joshua Von Nun. He never lay down for anybody; every Semite from Egypt to Assyria knew that. But here he is in submissive, profound worship of God.

Joshua here is the living illustration of what Paul calls for in Romans 12:1.

> I urge you therefore, brethren, by the mercies of God, to present your bodies a living and holy sacrifice, acceptable to God, which is your spiritual service of worship.

The root idea of "spiritual" or "reasonable" lies in the Greek word *logikos,* which carries the idea of logical.[4] Joshua's example and Paul's words tell us that total commitment is the only rational, logical course to take when we really see who God is. Nothing else makes any sense at all. To utterly submit is the only rational thing to do.

This reverent submission made Joshua eminently usable; because of it, he became the dread of the inhabitants of the land. The history of Israel reveals that every time they gave implicit, complete obedience to God, they were victorious.

The lesson of that moonlit night is clear for all of us: if we are to fight the battles of life successfully, we must be totally, worshipfully submitted. Sam Shoemaker said it perfectly—"To be a Christian means to give as much of myself as I can to as much of God as I know." Worshipful submission and commitment can turn us into modern Joshuas!

The Fourth Necessity: Reception of Guidance from God (6:2-5)

One final element is necessary for meeting the challenges that await us—and that is receiving divine direction from the

Lord. Human direction can have its drawbacks. A story was told in *Sunshine Magazine* about a family who had moved into a new neighborhood. One morning they overslept, and Jimmy, the youngest, missed his ride on the bus. His father offered to drive him to school, although he didn't know where it was located. So they started out, with Jimmy giving the directions. Going a few blocks, they made a left turn, then a right. As they continued along the route, they made several other turns. About twenty-five minutes later they finally arrived at their destination. Much to the father's amazement, the school was quite close to home. "Jimmy," he said, "how come you took me so far around?" His son replied rather apologetically, "I'm sorry, Dad. That's how our bus goes! It's the only way I know!"

Divine direction never fails, though at times it may not make any sense to human logic. God, the "captain of the host," was very clear in the directions which He gave to Joshua.

> And the Lord said to Joshua, "See, I have given Jericho into your hand, with its king and the valiant warriors. And you shall march around the city, all the men of war circling the city once. You shall do so for six days. Also seven priests shall carry seven trumpets of rams' horns before the ark; then on the seventh day you shall march around the city seven times, and the priests shall blow the trumpets. And it shall be that when they make a long blast with the ram's horn, and when you hear the sound of the trumpet, all the people shall shout with a great shout; and the wall of the city will fall down flat, and the people will go up every man straight ahead" (6:2-5).

These plans thoroughly contradicted human wisdom. Common-sense warfare required intelligent regimentation of the troops and specialization. They needed battering rams, scaling equipment, and other engines of war. Marching around the city could well leave them open to a murderous attack. And the imposed silence was absurd, especially when the marching warriors had to listen to the jeers of Jericho's Amorites. The plans God gave Joshua did not make any sense at all—according to human logic.

But Joshua believed! Hebrews 11:30 says, "By faith the

walls of Jericho fell down, after they had been encircled for seven days." It took great faith, for Joshua and company did, indeed, look absurd. It takes faith to follow God's directions for spiritual warfare. It takes faith not to "war according to the flesh" (2 Corinthians 10:3). It is by faith that we put on the belt of truth, the breastplate of righteousness, shoe our feet with the gospel, put on the helmet of salvation, and wield the sword of the Spirit, employing the ultimate weapon of prayer (cf. Ephesians 6:13-17). Following God's directions always takes faith, and it always pays off!

None of us will ever experience the kind of pressure Joshua knew that night as he meditated under the ramparts of Jericho, but we do face situations, personal Jerichos, which are more than we can handle. And Joshua's experience tells us what is spiritually necessary for the challenge.

> First, we need the revelation and realization that God is with us. We need to believe vividly that Christ is here. Our inner eye needs to see Him.
>
> Second, we need to realize that He bares the sword for His people, that He goes before. He will send legions of angels if it is necessary for His people, just as He did for that Indian pastor in the highlands of the Andes. Deborah sang of this in her song: "The stars fought from heaven, from their courses they fought against Sisera" (Judges 5:20).
>
> The third necessity is that we submit ourselves to Him in humble worship, for in submission lie elevation and power.
>
> Finally, we must follow the direction God gives, even if it means being thought foolish.

Rest in His presence. Believe it. See His sword bared for us. Fall in worshipful submission before Him and do what He says. And on the seventh day (the day of God's choice) the walls will come tumbling down.

Footnotes

1. C. F. Keil and F. Delitzsch, *Joshua, Judges, Ruth* (Grand Rapids: Eerdmans, 1963), p. 62.

2. John Calvin, *Commentaries on the Book of Joshua,* ed. note by Henry Beveridge (Grand Rapids: Baker, 1984), p. 88.
3. Charles Spurgeon, *The Metropolitan Tabernacle Pulpit,* Vol. 14 (Pasadena, Tex.: Pilgrim Publications, 1970), p. 88.
4. C. E. B. Cranfield, *Romans* (Edinburgh: T & T Clark, 1975), pp. 603-605.

7

FAITH'S FALLING WALLS

Joshua 6:1-27

The opening chapters of Joshua have presented an increasingly dramatic history, beginning with the amazing deliverance of the spies from Jericho and their optimistic report to Israel. This was followed by the Israelites' miraculous crossing of the Jordan and poignantly commemorated by the twelve stones set in the midst of Israel's first encampment at Gilgal. There in Gilgal Israel reaffirmed its covenantal relationship with God by circumcising all who were born in the wilderness and celebrating the Passover. Finally, in the ultimate prelude to the capture of Jericho, Joshua was confronted alone in the night by God Himself as the form of the sword-bearing "captain of the host," who completed his spiritual preparation for the impending conquest.

The following morning, as the bright rays of the early sun illuminated the thousands of orderly arranged tents of his people, Joshua knew what he had to do—and in the storied days that followed, he did it.

The writer of Hebrews tells us, in a simple sentence, that "By faith the walls of Jericho fell down, after they had been encircled for seven days" (Hebrews 11:30). This reference holds the key to the spiritual interpretation of the fall of Jericho: *the walls of Jericho fell because of the faith of Joshua and his people*. This display of faith, in fact, stands as the greatest thus far in the nation's history, one never to be exceeded. It is also highly significant because while the fall of Jericho is actual history, it is also a dramatized, extended parable about faith.

All of us can strengthen our own faith by observing the

dimensions of faith which Israel showed in conquering Jericho, and putting them to work in our own lives.

Faith's Factors: The Obedience of Faith

The first factor we see is obedience. The "captain of the host of the Lord"—the Lord Himself—gave *explicit* instructions to Joshua which demanded *implicit* obedience. Those instructions are detailed in verses 2-5, and then relayed to the people in verses 6-10. These instructions provide a precise outline for the order of the procession around Jericho. First come the soldiers, then seven priests carrying seven rams' horns or shofars; then comes the Ark on the shoulders of priests, then the people, and finally the rearguard.

What we should note here is that the Ark is in the *center* of the procession—dominating everything. We should also note that the seven priests with their seven shofar trumpets are meant to recall the seven days of God's work of creation. The Lord, who by His power created everything, would also use His power to bring them victory.[1]

The instructions are also explicit regarding what the forces of Israel must do. During the first six days they are to proceed *once* around the walled city each day, maintaining absolute silence while the priests blare intermittently on their shofars. On the seventh day they are to maintain the silence as they circle the walls *seven* times—until Joshua gives the command to "Shout!" (v. 10).

Here some observations are in order. First, from human experience, these instructions are absurd! The uniform witness of military history is that the foe is conquered by force. City walls are cleared by bombardment. Then they are scaled by ladder and rope. Gates are destroyed by battering rams. Troops are taken by sword. Cities do not fall before mystics making bad music on rams' horns.

We can be sure that when the Canaanites got a good look at the processional, they relaxed into incredulous catcalls and hoots. They could not believe their eyes. How ridiculous the Israelites looked.

Our second observation is that though the instructions were contrary to human logic, Israel believed. Why? Obviously because of their recent experience in watching the Jordan dry up when the Ark crossed its boundary. The freshness of that supreme miracle made them ready to believe. Another reason, less obvious, was the character and conviction of Joshua. Convinced of victory beyond any doubt, the general elevated the faith of his people through the intense sincerity of belief. Thus, Israel really did believe that God was going to give them Jericho. When the writer of Hebrews, under the inspiration of the Holy Spirit, says, "By faith the walls of Jericho fell down," he means they actually did have faith. They were not pretending, or trying to believe. They *did* believe! That is why they encircled the walls for seven days. That is why they were obedient.

A life of faith, then, is a life of obedience to God's direction, even when it seems absurd. In Judges 7 we see that Gideon beautifully demonstrated this when he faced his own enemies, a multitude of Midianites. At the beginning there were one hundred and thirty-five thousand Midianites (Judges 8:10) and thirty-two thousand Israelites (7:3). The Midianites outnumbered Israel four to one. The Lord did not think this match-up was very good, so He told Gideon to free all the soldiers from battle who wanted to leave. Twenty-two thousand departed, leaving ten thousand. Now the Midianites had a thirteen to one advantage. But God sought better odds, and, by having Gideon observe how each man drank from a stream, released all but three hundred soldiers (7:4–8). This was absurd. The match-up was four hundred and fifty to one!

But one dark night the three hundred surrounded the encamped Midianites, each armed with a candle, a pitcher, and a trumpet. At Gideon's signal they broke the pitchers, exposing the light, and blew their horns. The Midianites thought they were surrounded—and in the ensuing confusion fell upon each other, supposing their own countrymen to be the enemy. Gideon carried the day by slavishly adhering to the "absurd" directions of God!

God gives us directions in His Word as to how to meet the Jerichos, the challenges of our lives, and His directions are often absurd to human logic; but if we have faith, we will obey His directions. A man is filling out his income tax form and realizes that if he lists his extra hidden income, it will put him in a higher tax bracket and he will not have money to pay his taxes. He has a choice to make: do what is logical (as "everyone else does"), or be perfectly truthful, trusting God to take care of him.

A student is doing poorly in class. He needs a B to get into grad school, and he realizes there is no way as he works on his final exam. But he notices that his neighboring "A" student is working in such a way that he can read all his answers. What to do? Rationalize and say, "This is God's provision," or look back down to his own miserably empty paper, trusting God to work things out as He sees fit?

You have been wronged by an enemy. Now you have the chance to do him ill, and he will never know who did it. Everyone would applaud you for it, if they knew you did it. You know you can get away with it. But you also have the words of Jesus:

> You have heard that it was said, "YOU SHALL LOVE YOUR NEIGHBOR, AND HATE YOUR ENEMY." But I say to you, love your enemies, and pray for those who persecute you (Matthew 5:43, 44).

It is a spiritual law: disobedience reveals our unbelief; obedience reveals our faith. When difficult circumstances assail us, unbelief makes us borrow from the arsenals of the world, whereas faith causes us to take up the armor of God. Any Jerichos, threatening circumstances, facing you? Are you wavering between God's way and the world's? Do you believe God will deliver you? The authenticity of your belief will determine your obedience.

Israel Obeys

It was a little after dawn. The sun had lifted just above the horizon. Joshua had assembled his elders and given them the instructions from "the captain of the host." Now they were moving quickly throughout the camp, calling the people together. Soon a long procession began to wind from the camp. Though it was a vast number, it did not include all the people, but contained a delegation from each tribe. First were the men of war beneath their tribal banners; then seven white-robed priests, shofars in hand; in the center was the Ark; then more civilians and soldiers.

The procession made its way toward the city in absolute silence except for the discordant, elephantine blasts of the shofars. The trip from Gilgal around Jericho took about two hours, although Jericho was encircled in about twenty-five to thirty minutes. The Israelites stayed well beyond the range of Jericho's archers, but not beyond the taunts of the increasing number of her inhabitants who lined her walls. Yet Israel never broke silence. The procession continued in exactly the same way for six consecutive days. The Amorites had never seen anything like this. Though they shouted on, the grim silence of the Israelites began to wear on them.

Faith's Factors: Focus of Faith

The first great dimension of Israel's victorious faith is *obedience*. The second factor is the *focus* of Israel's faith.

The centerpiece of the narrative is the golden Ark of the Covenant—God's presence. The account mentions the Ark eleven times. The priests' horns bleated constantly to herald His presence, just as horns announced the appearance of God on Mt. Sinai (Exodus 19:16, 19; cf. also 2 Samuel 6:5). It was God's presence that encircled Jericho those seven days; it was His presence that would bring its fall.

Central to Israel's great experience of faith was the reality of God with them, leading them. We must emphasize that they were *not* imagining this. He was truly present! Of course He is everywhere; so logically the Ark could not go anywhere He was not present. But He manifested Himself specially through the Ark. The realization of His presence had a massive impact on the Israelites' faith.

So it is with us: if our eyes could be opened, even momentarily, to the spiritual presences in our own churches, we would never be the same. If, on a given Sunday morning, we suddenly had the ability to see the unseen, we would see angels moving about our sanctuaries. Perhaps we would discover that an angel sits next to us in human form as a "church visitor." Perhaps, if the preaching were "right on," the angels might listen intently, for Peter tells us that they "long to look" into spiritual truth (1 Peter 1:12). The Greek gives the idea of bending over or stooping to search the mysteries. The writer of Hebrews says, "Are they not all ministering spirits, sent out to render service for the sake of those who will inherit salvation?" (1:14).

If our eyes could be opened, we would say something very similar to what Jacob said at Bethel:

> Surely the Lord is in this place, and I did not know it. . . . How awesome is this place! This is none other than the house of God, and this is the gate of heaven (Genesis 28:16, 17).

Faith sees the presence of God when no one around does! Hebrews 11:1 says, "Now faith is the assurance of things hoped for, the conviction of things not seen." Faith sees many things that are unseen: angels, the promises of God, eternal realities. In 11:7 we see an aspect of the idea, where the writer says that Noah "saw" the Flood, yet unseen, because he believed God's word:

> By faith Noah, being warned by God about things not yet seen, in reverence prepared an ark for the salvation of his household, by which he condemned the world, and became an heir to the righteousness which is according to faith.

Hebrews 11:13 speaks of great men and women of faith seeing promises which they never received:

> All these died in faith, without receiving the promises, but having seen them and having welcomed them from a distance, and having confessed that they were strangers and exiles on the earth.

Hebrews 11:27 tells us that Moses saw God by faith: "By faith he left Egypt, not fearing the wrath of the king; for he endured, as seeing Him who is unseen."

As the Israelites encircled Jericho, the Canaanites saw nothing more than a ragtag people carrying a golden box, but the Israelites saw the unseen—they saw God and persisted to victory!

Faith's Factors: Dependence of Faith

Israel marched around Jericho thirteen times—once a day for six days and seven times on the seventh day (cf. v. 14). Why did God have them do this so many times? Perhaps in order to impress on their minds the futility of their situation. They saw that God would have to do it or it would never happen. As a result, they exercised their faith from a position of total dependence. They had no fortresses to which they could retreat. They lived in tents. They placed everything on the trustworthiness of God.

Rather than minimize the times when we must turn to Him, we need to welcome them as times to grow. God wants us to have a faith which is dependent as well as focused and obedient.

Faith's Factors: Declaration of Faith

It must have been very difficult for the Israelites to keep silent during those six days. Their enemies practiced no restraint—we can be sure of that. Moreover, not one stone in the walls had loosened, there were no cracks in the city "walled to the heavens," and the citizenry was far from saying "uncle." It must have been a great relief on the seventh day when Joshua ordered them to rise early and circle Jericho seven times, finishing with a great shout at his cue.

Verses 15-17 and 20 describe the climactic event:

> Then it came about on the seventh day that they rose early at the dawning of the day and marched around the city in the same manner seven times; only on that day they marched around the city seven times. And it came about at the seventh time, when the priests blew the trumpets, Joshua said to the people, "Shout! For the Lord has given you the city. And the city shall be under the ban, it and all that is in it belongs to the Lord; only Rahab the harlot and all who are with her in the house shall live, because she hid the messengers whom we sent. . . ."
>
> So the people shouted, and priests blew the trumpets; and it came about, when the people heard the sound of the trumpet, that the people shouted with a great shout and the wall fell down flat, so that the people went up into the city, every man straight ahead, and they took the city.

That shout was the voice of faith. It was the outward expression of the Israelites' inward confidence in the power of God. Faith declares itself. Faith that does not do so is not faith. Surely it was some shout! All their repressed Hebrew emotions came forth in a cry heard all the way to Gilgal and was no doubt answered! And the walls came tumbling down. Literally, "the wall fell in its place."

The collapse was complete, except for one small section from which a scarlet cord tossed in the wake of the concussion. It was the cord of faith. Hebrews 11:30, 31 tells us,

> By faith the walls of Jericho fell down, after they had been encircled for seven days. By faith Rahab the harlot did not perish along with those who were disobedient, after she had welcomed the spies in peace.

Faith Inside Jericho

During those last seven days all faith's factors, the dimensions of faith, had cycled through Rahab's growing soul. She gave implicit obedience to the explicit directions given her by God through the spies. She kept all her family in her home. Though some of them very likely questioned her wisdom, she did not capitulate but insisted that they remain. Her obedience bears testimony to an amazing faith. Rahab's obedience matched that of the encircling Israelites.

Day after day she rose to the trumpeting of the shofars as they announced the approach of God and the Ark, and peered out over her scarlet cord. The Israelites silently and knowingly stared back, and she rested her faith in the fact that God really was with them. It was the *focus* of faith. Perhaps she recited to her guests something of the testimony she had given to the spies:

> I know the Lord has given you the land. . . . For we have heard how the Lord dried up the water of the Red Sea before you when you came out of Egypt, and what you did to the two kings of the Amorites who were beyond the Jordan, to Sihon and Og, whom you utterly destroyed. And when we heard it, our hearts melted and no courage remained in any man any longer because of you; for the Lord your God, He is God in heaven above and on earth beneath (Joshua 2:9a, 10, 11).

By faith, like Noah and Moses before, Rahab saw the unseen. It changed her whole life.

Then there was the *dependence* of her faith. If Israel was defeated, her secret would become public and she would die miserably. It was all or nothing. Her faith was totally dependent. And she believed.

Finally, there was the *declaration,* the shout of faith. Earlier she had declared her faith to Israel's spies. And because of this she probably shouted out in concert with her new people, for faith declares itself.

True faith obeys God and His Word. True faith *focuses* upon God and sees the unseen. True faith *depends* upon God alone. True faith *declares* itself. How is your faith? How is the faith of the church? These things happened as an example for us who still fight the battles of faith. By learning from them, we too can achieve victory in the Lord, and He will cause impossible walls to tumble before us.

Footnotes

1. M. H. Woudstra, *The Book of Joshua* (Grand Rapids: Eerdmans, 1983), p. 110.

8

THE FOLLY OF HIDDEN SIN

Joshua 7:1-26

Chapter 7 of the Book of Joshua stands in marked contrast to chapter 6. While chapter 6 records a sublime victory, chapter 7 tells of a shameful defeat. Chapter 6 chronicles the factors of faith behind Israel's conquest of Jericho's impossible walls; chapter 7 describes the single factor underlying the Israelites' humiliating defeat by the much smaller army of Ai. Where chapter 6 is unforgettably positive, chapter 7 is memorably negative. Yet both are indispensable to understanding how we can successfully overcome the obstacles of life. Chapter 6 outlines what we must have to lead a victorious life, and chapter 7 tells us what we must *not* have: hidden sin.

The Committing of Hidden Sin (vv. 1, 21)

The story begins forthrightly with a concise description of the hidden sin:

> But the sons of Israel acted unfaithfully in regard to the things under the ban, for Achan, the son of Carmi, the son of Zabdi, the son of Zerah, from the tribe of Judah, took some of the things under the ban; therefore the anger of the Lord burned against the sons of Israel.

Verse 21, which records Achan's later confession, supplies more of the details.

> . . . when I saw among the spoil a beautiful mantle from Shinar and two hundred shekels of silver and a bar of gold fifty shekels in weight, then I coveted them and took them;

> and behold, they are concealed in the earth inside my tent with the silver underneath it.

Achan evidently belonged to the attack force which swept across the fallen walls of Jericho, conquered the people, collected the booty for the Lord's treasury, and burnt the city. He knew full well that the treasure from this first battle was banned from personal possession and consecrated to God (6:18, 19), but he simply could not resist. So, under the cover of the smoke and confusion of the burning city, he appropriated some gold and silver and a beautiful Babylonian coat, a "mantle from Shinar."

We can be fairly sure why Achan did this; he had already cultivated a taste for material things. Calvin notes from the later listing of Achan's oxen, donkeys, and sheep that he was already rich. Thus, not poverty, but a desire for luxury drove him to theft.[1] His pilfering of the luxurious imported Babylonian coat confirms this. Merchandise with a Babylonian origin was really "in." Babylon was one of the great cities of the world, and though at this time she was not at one of her zeniths, she remained culturally prominent. "Babylonian chic" was the thing! When Achan or his wife had an opportunity to wear this garment, heads would turn. The couple would be so cosmopolitan, so "Babylonian," so "vogue." Achan's theft revealed his yen for prestige and prominence. His sin was covetousness.

Achan's rationalization for breaking God's commandment came easily enough. No one would miss a couple of bars of silver and gold. And the coat? God did not wear coats—especially Babylonian coats. Besides, what he was doing would hurt no one. And no one would know anyway. How can any trouble come from something no one knows about?

Of course Achan was absolutely right—from ground level. No one knew anything, except perhaps his wife and children. His friends walked by his tent, even into it, and never suspected anything. But he forgot one thing: God knew! It is very human to think we can keep things to ourselves. Our son Carey thought so for a short time when he was about seven years old. We discovered this one day when my wife, cleaning out his drawer, found a pop can stuffed full of cigarette butts. Barbara and I checked his busy schedule and arranged a conference with him at our convenience! First question: why the cigarette butts? Answer: he and some of the other boys in his Sunday school class had collected them to smoke in secret. Second question: apart from the questionable practice of sucking on discarded cigarette butts extracted from the mire at the bottom of a dumpster, didn't he realize his secret smoking was wrong? I will never forget his answer, for he said, "I didn't think it was wrong because you didn't know." What a wonderful way to make your preacher-father's day. "It is not wrong if no one knows." We chuckle at it now, for his short-lived assumption was simply what one of the boys reassuringly said to the group when they expressed their reservations—and Carey picked it up as gospel.

We may laugh at that, but his delusion demonstrates in miniature how thousands of people like Achan regard their personal lives. "It is not wrong if no one knows about it and it does not hurt others." What they forget is that God knows *everything*. The Scriptures are explicit:

> Thou dost understand my thought from afar. Thou dost scrutinize my path and my lying down, and art intimately acquainted with all my ways. Even before there is a word on my tongue, behold, O Lord, Thou dost know it all (Psalm 139:24).
>
> And there is no creature hidden from His sight, but all things are open and laid bare to the eyes of Him with whom we have to do (Hebrews 4:13).

We do nothing that God does not know about. No night is too dark, no mine too deep, no galaxy too distant for Him to know every thought and every action. God knew Achan's covetous thoughts long before they led to his thievery. The internalization of this truth is so healthy, for when we truly believe it, it motivates us to guard not only our actions but our thoughts. Believing that He knows every nuance of our minds has a way of elevating our thoughts.

Achan thought he was committing a hidden sin that even God did not see. He also thought that it would not hurt anyone else. But how pitifully wrong he was on both counts!

The Results of Hidden Sin (vv. 2-9)

Achan's hidden sin had two effects among his people—first defeat, and then discouragement. Verses 2-5 describe their pitiful defeat:

> Now Joshua sent men from Jericho to Ai, which is near Beth-aven, east of Bethel, and said to them, "Go up and spy out the land." So the men went up and spied out Ai. And they returned to Joshua and said to him, "Do not let all the people go up; only about two or three thousand men need go up to Ai; do not make all the people toil up there, for they are few." So about three thousand men from the people went up there, but they fled from the men of Ai. And the men of Ai struck down about thirty-six of their men, and pursued them down on the descent, so the hearts of the people melted and became as water.

Buoyant and optimistic after their effortless defeat of Jericho, the spies returned recommending that only two or three thousand soldiers would be needed to take Ai. Joshua, just to be safe, sent the larger number of three thousand to do the job. Very likely the soldiers marched up gaily to battle while thousands of their light-hearted comrades waved and cheered—much as the crowds cheered the Doughboys in World War I. But the slender forces of Ai did not lie down as expected; they withstood the Israelites to the point of chasing them to Shebarim, where thirty-six men of Israel died. The heady emotion of the victory over Jericho was erased in a few moments, and the heart of the people melted.

The dismay of the people spread to Joshua himself, who fell briefly to a disillusioned loss of faith, as verses 6-9 reveal:

> Then Joshua tore his clothes and fell to the earth on his face before the ark of the Lord until the evening, both he and the elders of Israel; and they put dust on their heads. And Joshua said, "Alas, O Lord God, why didst Thou ever bring this people over to Jordan, only to deliver us into the hand of the Amorites, to destroy us? If only we had been willing to dwell beyond the Jordan! Oh Lord, what can I say since Israel has turned their back before their enemies? For the Canaanites and all the inhabitants of the land will hear of it,

> and they will surround us and cut off our name from the earth. And what wilt Thou do for Thy great name?"

Joshua, unaware of Achan's sin, ironically speaks in tones of complaint and unbelief. In fact, he ironically uses language very similar to that used by the unbelieving Israelites thirty-eight years earlier when they rejected his and Caleb's advice that they could take the Promised Land (see Exodus 14:2, 3). Achan's hidden sin not only brought defeat to his people, but caused Joshua (one of the greatest men ever!) to fall to despair and momentary lapse of faith.

The primary message of this passage is: hidden sin always brings defeat and discouragement to God's people. This happens because believers have a profound solidarity with one another. God's covenant people were knit together by a mystical bond so truly real that none of them lived and died to themselves. Gerhard Von Rad, the eminent Old Testament theologian, says that the Bible, properly understood, does not teach individualism anywhere.[2] Old Testament history continuously affirms the solidarity of God's people.

The New Testament descriptions of the church carry the idea to even greater heights.

> For even as the body is one and yet has many members, and all the members of the body, though they are many, are one body, so also is Christ. For by one Spirit we were all baptized into one body, whether Jews or Greeks, whether slaves or free, and we were all made to drink of one Spirit. For the body is not one member, but many (1 Corinthians 12:12-14).

> And He put all things in subjection under his feet, and gave Him as head over all things to the church, which is His body, the fullness of Him who fills all in all (Ephesians 1:22, 23).

As we live out our lives in this world, we are not like so many marbles bouncing off each other, influencing one another by occasional bumps. Rather, we are like fruit on the vine drawing from and contributing to each other's lives. When one of us leads a virtuous, productive life, it has a way of elevating us all; but when one fails, it also pulls us down.

Outward sin or outward virtues of other believers dramatically affect us. We know what would happen to our church if the pastors or the elders fell into grievous public sin. In fact, we are all too well aware of what it is doing to the church across America today. We understand the detrimental effects of outward sin.

But the question is, how do the hidden sins—the sins others know nothing about—how do these hidden sins affect other believers? The answer is this: so-called hidden sins lead to a deterioration of character, reducing the ring of truth and reality of what we say and do. For example, I may give assent to the doctrines of the church. I may even teach them. I may be an elder or a preacher. I also may *not* be committing any outward sins—those that others can see. But if I am inwardly a sensualist, or a thief, or a bigot, or a gossip—then my ethos, what I am, will suffer a reduction in authenticity. And any reduction in my authenticity will have a telling effect on the church. The hidden sins of God's people are what destroy so many today. The mental adulterer, the secret gossiper, the covertly hateful, the covetous *reduce themselves* and thereby bring defeat and discouragement to the church. Often their children fall away, and their business acquaintances and neighbors have no desire for their Christianity.

How we live inwardly, how we conduct ourselves when no one we know is around, brings either victory and enthusiasm, or defeat and discouragement to the church.

God does not bless the life in which there is hidden sin; and God does not bless the church in which there is hidden sin. Achan's hidden sin was not hidden to God. His sin brought defeat and discouragement to God's people.

The Discovery of Hidden Sin (vv. 10-23)

Now Achan's sin is found out. Verses 10-12 record God's words as he commanded Joshua to stand before Him and then revealed the nature of the problem, telling Joshua that Israel would continue in defeat unless the stolen articles were purged. Then, in verses 13-15, he informed Joshua of the process for finding the culprit. It was a dramatic process which involved the casting of lots. God required it for two reasons: first, to publicly emphasize the horror of inward sin; and secondly, to underline the fact that one person's inward sin can bring defeat to God's people. Verses 16-18 describe the process:

> So Joshua arose early in the morning and brought Israel near by tribes, and the tribe of Judah was taken. And he brought the families of Judah near, and he took the family of Zerahites; and he brought the family of Zerahites near man by man, and Zabdi was taken. And he brought his household near man by man; and Achan, son of Carmi, son of Zabdi, son of Zerah, from the tribe of Judah was taken.

We can all feel with Achan. His heart began to violently throb when he heard that Joshua was going to muster the people the next morning. Sleep was impossible, and he was among the first to see the blush of the rising sun across the Jordan. As the tribe of Judah was singled out, he felt his stomach contract. When the next lot narrowed the offender down to the descendants of his great-grandfather, Zerah, he felt faint, and a terrible darkness engulfed him. Then, as his grandfather's children were called forth, his knees buckled. And when his name was finally sounded, everything became a terrible blur.

There Achan stood before Joshua, the elders, and all the nation—as far as his blinking eyes could see.

> Then Joshua said to Achan, "My son, I implore you, give glory to the Lord, the Lord of Israel, and give praise to Him; and tell me now what you have done. Do not hide it."

Joshua called him "My son" neither ironically nor hypocritically. Achan had sinned greatly, and he was going to have to pay the price, but Joshua was compassionate. Achan could stand it no longer and poured forth his confession in simple truth:

> So Achan answered Joshua and said, "Truly, I have sinned against the Lord, the God of Israel, and this is what I did; when I saw among the spoil a beautiful mantle from Shinar and two hundred shekels of silver and a bar of gold fifty shekels in weight, then I coveted them and took them; and behold, they are concealed in the earth inside my tent with the silver underneath it."

He called his actions what they were—sin. He described the pattern of his fall using three verbs: *saw, coveted, took*. They are the same three words used to describe Eve's fall in Genesis 3:6,and the words which encompass David's sin in 2 Samuel 11. Achan told the truth, and it is verified not only by historical archetype but also by our human experience.

Here we see Achan's redemption. He was going to die terribly. He had sinned against God and against his own people. Their blood cried out. But he had confessed. He had, like David, confessed that his sin was against God (see Psalm 51:3, 4) and he was transparently honest. He offered no excuses. Proverbs 28:13 says, "He who conceals his trangressions will not prosper, but he who confesses and forsakes them will find compassion." Achan confessed his sin. His remaining moments afforded him no opportunity to demonstrate his repentance. I believe he was saved, "yet by fire." And this is what the ancient Jewish sages also believed.[3]

The lesson is there for us. The remedy for hidden sin is confession. The Apostle John tells us,

> If we say that we have no sin we are deceiving ourselves, and the truth is not in us. If we confess our sins, He is faithful and righteous to forgive us our sins and to cleanse us from all unrighteousness (1 John 1:8, 9).

The offer of confession and forgiveness comes because Christ took our sins on Himself. "He made Him who knew no sin to be sin on our behalf, that we might become the righteousness of God in Him" (2 Corinthians 5:21). If we confess our hidden sins to Jesus, He will forgive us willingly and joyfully.

The Punishment of Hidden Sin (vv. 24-26)

First came the committing of hidden sin, then the results of hidden sin, next the discovery of hidden sin, and now the punishment of hidden sin.

> Then Joshua and all Israel with him, took Achan the son of Zerah, the silver, the mantle, the bar of gold, his sons, his daughters, his oxen, his donkeys, his sheep, his tent and all that belonged to him and they brought them up to the valley of Achor. And Joshua said, "Why have you troubled us? The

> Lord will trouble you this day." And all Israel stoned them with stones, and they burned them with fire after they had stoned them with stones. And they raised over him a great heap of stones that stands to this day, and the Lord turned from the fierceness of His anger. Therefore the name of that place has been called the valley of Achor to this day.

Achan's family, evidently guilty of complicity in his sin, shared the horrible punishment. Here God had Israel raise another mound of "stones of remembrance." The twelve stones in the Jordan and in Gilgal were to remind them of His power to deliver. Here a massive pile of thousands of stones reminded Israel never again to imagine that hidden sin would go unnoticed or unpunished.

The stones of remembrance call us to self-examination. Is there hidden sin in our lives?

Footnotes

1. John Calvin, *Commentaries on the Book of Joshua* (Grand Rapids: Baker, 1984), p. 118.
2. Gerhard Von Rad, *Old Testament Theology,* Vol. I, trans. D. M. G. Stalker (New York: Harper & Row, 1962), pp. 265-268.
3. Louis Ginzberg, *The Legends of the Jews,* Vol. 4 (Philadelphia: The Jewish Publication Society, 1954), p. 8. "This determined Achan to confess his sins. The confession cost him his life, but it saved him from losing his share in the world to come."

9

THE SERIOUSNESS OF SIN
Joshua 8:1-35

On the surface it would be very natural to ask why Joshua 8, the record of Israel's bloody annihilation of the inhabitants of Ai, is in the Bible. How can we possibly benefit from learning how the Israelites accomplished genocide in the cities of Ai and Bethel? Having now studied it, I believe that the answer is this: God is very concerned about the purity of His people—and He wants us to understand just how important purity is. He also wants us to know (and this is His primary concern) that His holiness and glory are more important than anything else.

In a sentence, the destruction of Ai and the ritual that followed at Mount Ebal teach us some much-needed lessons about the mind and heart of God and what He expects of us. Sometimes these so-called "difficult passages" are far more profitable than they might appear at first glance. Studying them both challenges and illuminates us, because they lead to a better understanding of God, of ourselves, and of the seriousness of sin.

The Annihilation of Ai (vv. 1-29)

Israel had just suffered a humiliating loss to the inferior forces of Ai because of Achan's hidden sin. Achan and his family had been judged, and now God called the Israelites to attack Ai again. But this time He called all the shots. First, He told Joshua to take thirty thousand soldiers and send them by night on a thirteen-mile journey to the west side of the city, where they would lie in ambush (vv. 3, 4). The next day he was to take the main army up to the north side of Ai (v. 11) and then send a detachment of five thousand to guard his flank from Bethel and also wait in ambush.

The plan worked perfectly. The main army beseiged Ai and then feigned retreat, thus drawing the foolish Amorites out of the city in reckless pursuit. Once they were beyond the gates, Joshua raised his javelin as a signal and the thirty thousand who lay in wait overran the city and set it on fire (vv. 18-20). Evidently the five thousand encountered some resistance from Bethel but also overran it (cf. v. 17). And the holocaust was assured. The inhabitants of the city had nowhere to turn. They were surrounded on every side. Verses 24, 25 record their terrible *terminus ad quem:*

> Now it came about when Israel had finished killing all the inhabitants of Ai in the field in the wilderness where they pursued them, and all of them were fallen by the edge of the sword until they were destroyed, then all Israel returned to Ai and struck it with the edge of the sword. And all who fell that day, both men and women, were 12,000—all the people of Ai.

Every living soul—the young, the old, the pregnant woman, the nursing mother—was stabbed and hacked to death, and the bodies burned in the flames that engulfed the city. No soul received mercy—not even the infants. Joshua kept his javelin aloft until every heart ceased to beat.

The king was captured alive and hung in a nearby tree to symbolize his cursedness (Deuteronomy 21:22, 23), but taken down at night in accordance with Jewish law. In a final indignity, the soldiers of Israel threw his body forth at the gate of the city where he had once sat on his throne as judge, and raised a great heap of stones over it (v. 29). The whole thing is ghastly. None of us can imagine ourselves participating in such a thing—flaying away at the helpless bodies of women and children until at last they made no sound. The horror is beyond words. Fortunately, none of us can ever be called to do such a thing. We have the example of the cross and the victory of the resurrection of Christ. We are enjoined not to fight for the faith with the weapons of this world, as Paul tells us in 2 Corinthians 10:4, 5: ". . . for the weapons of our warfare are not of the flesh, but divinely powerful for the destruction of fortresses."

The Old Testament Is Violent

Nevertheless, the Old Testament remains a bloody book—and it is bloody in obedience to God! King Saul suffered the loss of his throne because he did not completely exterminate the Amalekites as God commanded, but allowed King Agag to live. Samuel's word to him was:

> I will not return with you, for you have rejected the word of the Lord, and the Lord has rejected you from being king over Israel (1 Samuel 15:26).

Verses 32, 33 reveal the Lord's solution:

> Then Samuel said, "Bring me Agag, the king of the Amalekites." And Agag came to him cheerfully. And Agag said, "Surely the bitterness of death is past." But Samuel said, "As your sword has made women childless, so shall your mother be childless among women." And Samuel hewed Agag to pieces before the Lord in Gilgal.

It was in obedience to God that the entire populations of Makkedah (10:28), Lachish (v. 32), Eglon (v. 35), Debir (v. 39), and all the cities in the Negev and the Shephelah were put to death (v. 40). In the northern campaign Israel thoroughly destroyed Hazor, Madon, Shemron and Achshaph (Joshua 11:11-14). The story of the conquest of Palestine is truly terrible!

Because of this bloody record, the nineteenth-century liberals began to reject the Old Testament. They considered it crude, primitive, out of keeping with their modern sentiments. Schleiermacher, the eighteenth- and nineteenth-century father of liberalism, said that the Old Testament has a place in the Christian heritage only by virtue of its connections with Christianity. He felt that it should be no more than an appendix of historical interest. Adolph Harnack argued that the Reformers should have dropped it from the canon of authoritative writings. Likewise, there are thousands today who have rejected the Old Testament either formally or in practice.

The error of this kind of approach was pointed out by a fellow liberal, Albert Schweitzer, who showed that such thinking amounts to choosing the things about God which fit man-made theology. Men project their own thoughts about God back up to God and create a god of their own thinking. Men "civilize" God and make Him, according to their own thoughts, a "nice guy." God becomes captive to their thoughts. But I must say, hopefully without being misunderstood, that God is *not* civilized. He cannot be tamed by our humanistic thinking.

God Is Just

We will return to this point shortly, but first we should note that there are a number of reasons from which we may conclude that God's judgment of the Canaanites was not unjust.

First, He had been amazingly patient with them. Four hundred years before, when God was affirming His covenant with Abraham, He told how the Jews would be captive in Egypt and would not return until the fourth generation—His explanation being,

> Then in the fourth generation they shall return here, for the iniquity of the Amorites is not yet full (Genesis 15:16).

God had been amazingly patient. The cup of the Amorites had been filling and filling—yet He withheld judgment in His forbearance. But then their cup was full, and He came with the Israelites in judgment. The story of Sodom and Gomorrah is a similar study in divine forbearance. The entire populace practiced aggressive homosexuality and murder. Yet when Abraham pleaded with God to spare Sodom, the dialogue revealed Him willing to spare the people for the sake of fifty righteous, then forty-five, even forty, then thirty, then twenty, then ten. Not even ten righteous could be found! Their cup was full; through overflowing wickedness, they brought on themselves the fire and brimstone of a volcanic eruption. This destruction of Sodom and Gomorrah was an early stroke of the holy sword, which came down in a wider area when the Amorites' cup brimmed over. We must thus see the destruction of Ai against the backdrop of God's amazingly gracious patience.

Second, we must note the depravity of the Canaanites. Their sensuality was proverbial. David Hubbard says, in his *New Bible Dictionary* article on the Canaanites, "That Canaanite religion appealed to the bestial and material in human nature is clearly evidenced by the Ugaritic texts. . . ."[1] Much of their statuary is pornographic. In addition they regularly practiced child sacrifice, as the foundation sacrifices uncovered at Gezer illustrate.[2]

Third, when the Israelites did not obey God and exterminate the Canaanites, the Canaanites did, indeed, pollute Israel. The kings of Judah practiced child sacrifice (2 Kings 16:3; 21:6). There also came perversion of sexual relations in the name of religion (2 Kings 23:7). Furthermore, the Israelites took up magic and necromancy (2 Kings 21:6), and finally murdered the prophets of God (Jeremiah 26:20-23). When King Balak sought advice from Balaam on how to curse the Jews, Balaam advised intermarriage. The sad success of his advice is recorded in Numbers 31:15-20. Israel suffered continual contamination from the Canaanites.

Lastly, we must realize that whenever a people's cup becomes full, the judgment comes. In Noah's day, when God saw that "every intent of the thoughts of (man's) heart was only evil continually" (Genesis 6:5), He judged the people with a flood. Likewise, in Sodom He judged them with volcanic fire. And here He judged them by the sword of Israel. One day Christ will come back personally, riding on a white horse, His eyes flames of fire, His head crowned with many diadems, His body clothed in a robe dipped in blood—and He will judge the earth, for its cup will be full (cf. Revelation 19:11-16).

So for these reasons—the Canaanites' depravity, their ability to pollute Israel, God's incredible patience, and His resolve to punish when the cup is full—we must never fall to the foolishness of supposing God unjust in judging the Canaanites.

The more we study this gory eighth chapter of Joshua the more we understand why it is in the Bible, for it teaches us some essential truths about God. It teaches us that there are some things more important than human life—namely, God's holiness and the holiness of His people. God matters more than you or I! Aware of that vital point, St. Anselm, Anselm of Canterbury, posed this question:

> If you should find yourself in the sight of God and one said to you: "Look thither"; and God on the other hand, should say:

> "It is not my will that you should look"; ask your own heart what there is in all existing things which would make it right for you to give that look contrary to the will of God.

Anselm's reply is, "I must confess that I ought not to oppose the will of God even to preserve the whole creation. . . ."[3]

Using the more extreme illustration, Anselm tells us the truth: even if he could save all creation by opposing God's will, he would not do it, because God's glory and honor outweigh all human life and all creation! If we do not like this, it is because our world has trained us to see man as the measure of all things. We must fix in our hearts this reality—*God's holiness is more important than man's life.*

We must also understand that God is not like us. He is other. We must resist with all our might the mistake of those nineteenth-century theologians who attempted to tame God, to make Him our nice, safe neighbor who passes no moral judgments. Remember the conversation between Lucy and Mr. and Mrs. Beaver in *The Lion, the Witch, and the Wardrobe*?

> "Is—is he a man?" asked Lucy.
>
> "Aslan a man!" said Mr. Beaver sternly. "Certainly not. I tell you he is the King of the wood and the son of the great Emperor-Beyond-the Sea. Don't you know who is the King of Beasts? Aslan is a lion—*the* Lion, the great Lion."
>
> "Oooh!" said Susan. "I'd thought he was a man. Is he—quite safe? I shall feel rather nervous about meeting a lion."
>
> "That you will, dearie, and no mistake," said Mrs. Beaver, "if there's anyone who can appear before Aslan without their knees knocking, they're either braver than most or else just silly."
>
> "Then he isn't safe?" said Lucy.
>
> "Safe?" said Mr. Beaver. "Don't you hear what Mrs. Beaver tells you? Who said anything about safe? Course he isn't safe."[4]

God isn't like us! May we, as well as our children, keep this in mind.

We must also remember that God's thoughts and actions sometimes extend beyond and are contrary to our finite reasoning.

> For My thoughts are not your thoughts, neither are your ways My ways, declares the Lord. For as the heavens are higher than the earth, so are My ways higher than your ways, and My thoughts than your thoughts (Isaiah 55:8, 9).

The eighth chapter of Joshua teaches us that God is a God who judges. God sheds human blood for certain reasons. Sacred history shows beyond a shadow of a doubt that when man's cup is full, wrath comes. Any sensitive person must wonder about our cup in the modern Western world which must surely be almost full—if we look to the lesson of this chapter.

The Old and New Testaments give us a full portrait of God. To dwell exclusively on the Old or the New is like tearing a photograph in half. We will only see Him for what He truly is when we bring the two pieces together. God deliver us from the tame God of our imaginations.

The gory, smoking stones of Ai were meant to be a great visual lesson both to Israel and to the Canaanites. But God especially wanted to drive the point home to His own people. Many readers believe what follows to be the very summit of all the Book of Joshua—even more significant than the crossing of the Jordan. It is the building of an altar and the proclamation of the Law, described in verse 30 and following: "Then Joshua built an altar to the Lord, the God of Israel, in Mount Ebal."

The Building of an Altar to God (vv. 30-35)

Mount Ebal and Mount Gerizim were about fifteen miles from Gilgal; so when we read that Israel traveled to Ebal, we must imagine it took the multiple hundreds of thousands about two days to assemble there. Actually they congregated in the small Valley of Shechem, formed by the depression between Mount Ebal on the north and Mount Gerizim on the south. The slopes of the two valleys join to create a magnificent natural amphitheatre.

There, according to verse 31, they built

> . . . an altar of uncut stones, on which no man had wielded an iron tool, and they offered burnt offerings on it to the Lord, and sacrificed peace offerings (cf. Exodus 20:24-26).

It was a spectacular scene; the valley itself was known for its verdant, grassy beauty, and the massed thousands of Israelites, in their bright colors, would naturally have spread out along the surrounding slopes to see the altar built. They all knew the significance of the event, for this was the first altar built in the Promised Land—and it was made in fulfillment of Moses' specific directions (Deuteronomy 27). The altar was constructed of uncut stones because God did not dwell in a Temple made with hands. The Lord's people wanted no part in idolatrous worship.

The "burnt offering" was thoroughly consumed by fire, signifying the complete presentation of oneself to the Lord. It was the model for Paul's words in Romans 12:1,

> I urge you therefore, brethren, by the mercies of God, to present your bodies a living and holy sacrifice, acceptable to God, which is your spiritual service of worship.

It meant total commitment, total self-giving. By this token, Israel committed itself wholly to God.

The "peace offering" was not completely burnt, for it constituted a type of communion meal. The fat was burnt on the altar to suggest God's part of the meal; the people who offered it ate the rest. This *shalom* offering symbolized wholeness and well-being in the people's solidarity with God. It was a celebration characterized by joy. Moses said of it,

> You shall build the altar of the Lord your God of uncut stones; and you shall offer on it burnt offerings to the Lord your God; and you shall sacrifice peace offerings and eat there, and you shall rejoice before the Lord your God (Deuteronomy 27:6, 7).

It is an idyllic image—the hosts of Israel repeatedly sacrificing to God on the altar of uncut stones[5]—as the aroma of the offering permeates the beautiful valley.

The scene increases in dramatic intensity as Israel moved beyond the offerings to do something it had never done before. Verse 32 mentions it only briefly.

> And he wrote there on the stones a copy of the Law of Moses, which he had written in the presence of the sons of Israel.

Moses' original instructions about the writing in Deuteronomy 27:1–8 give us the details:

> Then Moses and the elders of Israel charged the people, saying, "Keep all the commandments which I command you today. So it shall be on the day when you shall cross the Jordan to the land which the Lord your God gives you, that you shall set up for yourself large stones, and coat them with lime and write on them all the words of this law, when you cross over, in order that you may enter the land which the Lord your God gives you, a land flowing with milk and honey, as the Lord, the God of your fathers, promised you. So it shall be when you cross the Jordan, you shall set up on Mount Ebal these stones, as I am commanding you today, and you shall coat them with lime. . . . And you shall write on the stones all the words of this law very distinctly."

The method of plastering stones and then printing on them came originally from Egypt; thus, the letters were probably painted in red. So we can imagine large whitewashed monoliths with red Hebrew characters spelling out the Ten Commandments, and possibly the blessings and curses of the Law as well (cf. Deuteronomy 28). This structure was the *first* public display of the Law. Its words, no longer the exclusive treasure of God's people, became public information, announcing to the nations what God requires of all people. Calvin says,

> This made it palpable even to strangers entering the land what God was worshipped in it, and all excuse for error was taken away.[6]

The solemn monoliths set amidst the thousands in Shechem made quite a sight.

Blessings and Cursings

But what took place around these stones of the Law is still more dramatic—truly unforgettable. All Israel—men, women, children—were divided into two massive groups, each numbering several hundred thousand.

Deuteronomy 27:12, 13 tells of Moses' command that the tribes of Simeon, Levi, Judah, Issachar, Joseph, and Benjamin terrace themselves on the slopes of Mount Gerizim—"to bless the people." On Mount Ebal were stationed the tribes of Reuben, Gad, Asher, Zebulun, Dan, and Naphtali, "for the curse." In the valley, among all the white-robed Levites assembled around the altar and the great white stones, lay the gleaming Ark of the Covenant. The Ark was the very center and focus of everything; the Lord's people surrounded His presence on all sides.

With everyone in place, Joshua led a great antiphonal chant based on the list of the blessings and the curses that accompany obedience or disobedience to the Lord (cf. Deuteronomy 27:11—28:6). Joshua, and perhaps the Levites in chorus, shouted aloud, "Cursed is he who dishonors his father or mother." Then a tremendous "Amen!"—a hundred-fold louder—rose from the thousands on the slopes of Ebal and thundered across to Gerizim, echoing back again. One after another the curses were read, each followed by a roaring "Amen!" Then the blessings were intoned, and the slopes of Gerizim roared an even louder "Amen!" because the tribes were larger. "Amen! Amen! Amen! Amen!" Surely this must have been one of the greatest spectacles the world has ever seen.

Some Abiding Lessons

Now put it all together: the still smoldering ruins of Ai and Jericho; the terrible heaps of stones of judgment over their depraved sovereigns; the mystic stone monoliths which proclaim in red the standards for God's people; and then the people thundering, cursing themselves if they did not follow the Law, blessing themselves if they did. The point is clear—God is a holy God who hates sin and judges it!

Our Jesus of the New Testament is the God who judged Ai, the God who put every man, woman, and child to the sword. When He ordered the extermination of the Amorites, He was "the Lamb slain before the foundation of the world." He had already covenanted to die for His people. This same Jesus who destroyed Ai died on the cross for the sins of the world, and will return with a sword, wearing a robe soaked with the blood of His enemies. The Jesus of the New Testament did not evolve from the God of the Old Testament. He has never changed; He never will. "Jesus Christ is the same yesterday and today and forever" (Hebrews 13:8).

We must bring all the revelation concerning God together. We must read the passages which teach His sacrificial love alongside the passages which teach His implacable wrath. To do otherwise means creating a God of our own imagination. We must revel in the divine paradox, for in it we learn the deepest truth.

The Father, the Son, and the Holy Spirit hate sin and are going to judge the world. One day, if there is no repentance, the cup of the West will be full. How can it be otherwise for a culture that spends billions on pornography? How can it be otherwise for a society which sacrifices its unborn to the altars of comfort and convenience? Beyond a shadow of doubt, a day of judgment is coming unless we undergo a national repentance.

Chapter 8 of Joshua calls us to take sin seriously. Jesus took it so seriously that He judged Ai. He took it so seriously that He died on the cross for it. We must also take it seriously. We are to flee it and fight it, to repent of it, to pray for deliverance from it.

If we are believers, we are washed in the blood of Christ. But that does not free us from the obligation to examine our lives and see what is in our hearts, to confess our sin. God does not take sin lightly. He judges it. May we hear the Word of God and open ourselves to His whole counsel. May we understand God as He is, fall down before Him as a holy God, and do homage to Him—with all of our hearts, with all of our will, with everything that is within us.

Footnotes

1. J. D. Douglas, ed., *The New Bible Dictionary* (Grand Rapids: Eerdmans, 1962), p. 186.
2. James Orr, ed., *The International Standard Bible Encyclopedia,* Vol. 1 (Grand Rapids: Eerdmans, 1939), pp. 550, 551.
3. St. Anselm, *Cur Deus Homo,* Vol. X (Library of Christian Classics edition), p. 1098.

4. C. S. Lewis, *The Lion, the Witch, and the Wardrobe* (Collins, 1974), p. 77.
5. The January-February 1985 issue of *Biblical Archaeological Review* (Vol. 22, No. 1) carries an article by Adam Zartel entitled "Has Joshua's Altar Been Found at Mount Ebal?" which by means of beautiful photographs and clear exposition demonstrates the likelihood of its having been unearthed. Zartel writes with scientific restraint: "We have on Mt. Ebal not only the complete prototype of an Israelite altar, but moreover, a site that might prove to be directly related to the Biblical traditions concerning Joshua's building of an altar on Mt. Ebal" (pp. 26-43).
6. John Calvin, *Commentaries on the Book of Joshua* (Grand Rapids: Baker, 1984), p. 133.

10

WHEN LEADERSHIP FAILS
Joshua 9:1-27

In that glorious assembly on the slopes of Ebal and Gerizim, Israel renewed her covenantal commitment to God and reacknowledged the seriousness of sin. No one among the hosts of Israel would ever forget that day—especially their impressionable children. The lesson was meant to last.

With the ceremony completed, Israel returned past the charred ruins of Ai and Jericho to their base camp at Gilgal, where they prepared themselves for the Canaanite campaign.

Meanwhile, the inhabitants of the land geared up for the coming assault by forming a confederacy, described in verses 1 and 2:

> Now it came about when all the kings who were beyond the Jordan, in the hill country and lowland and on all the coast of the Great Sea toward Lebanon, the Hittite and the Amorite, the Canaanite, the Perizzite, the Hivite and the Jebusite, heard of it, that they gathered themselves together with one accord to fight with Joshua and with Israel.

These military allies hoped to withstand the invading hordes. But the Gibeonites, a branch of the Hivites who occupied the four sister cities of Gibeon, Chephirah, Beeroth, and Kiriath-jearim (9:17), saw it differently. They believed that the transcending God of Israel stood so strongly with His people that all the land would fall (9:24). They also saw that they were next in line after Jericho and Ai.

So, in desperation, they concocted a clever plan. It began with brilliantly conceived costuming: scruffy, bedraggled donkeys bore worn-out sacks which had been patched and re-patched; weary-looking tribesmen carried goat wineskins, shriveled by the sun, torn, stitched, and rebound; on their feet hung shredded, unserviceable sandals; old, faded, ragged robes barely shielded them from the hot sun. They brought with them sacks of dry, moldy bread, crumbling to the touch. What a sight they were—covered with the supposed dust of a thousand miles, dirty, smelly. It was an impeccable disguise.

And their script was perfect. *The Living Bible* records it as follows in verses 8-13:

> "But who are you?" Joshua demanded. "Where do you come from?" And they told him, "We are from a very distant country; we have heard of the might of the Lord your God and of all that he did in Egypt, and what you did to the two kings of the Amorites—Sihon, king of Heshbon, and Og, king of Bashan. So our elders and our people instructed us, 'Prepare for a long journey; go to the people of Israel and declare our nation to be their servants, and ask for peace.' This bread was hot from the ovens when we left, but now as you see, it is dry and moldy; these wineskins were new, but now they are old and cracked; our clothing and shoes have become worn out from our long, hard trip."

Their story was so reasonable, their references to Jehovah so reverential, and their appearance so in keeping with their story that the leadership of Israel was completely taken in. And thus we have the fateful words of verses 14 and 15:

> So the men of Israel took some of their provisions, and did not ask for the counsel of the Lord. And Joshua made a covenant with them, to let them live; and the leaders of the congregation swore an oath to them.

Joshua made *shalom* with the Gibeonites. He vowed friendship with his enemies and the enemies of God!

His covenant with these Hivites was in direct disobedience to the words of Moses in Deuteronomy 7:1, 2:

> When the Lord your God shall bring you into the land where you are entering to possess it, and shall clear away many nations before you, the Hittites and the Girgashites and the Amorites and the Canaanites and the Perizzites and the Hi-

> vites and the Jebusites, seven nations greater and stronger than you; and when the Lord your God shall deliver them before you, and you shall defeat them, then you shall utterly destroy them. You shall make no covenant with them and show no favor to them.

Joshua and his leaders, who had been riding a spectacular series of successes, suddenly suffered an immense lapse of spiritual leadership.

Why did Joshua fail? What did he and his elders do to make it "right"? What did God ultimately do? In answering these questions, the ninth chapter of Joshua provides us with an anatomy of failure in spiritual leadership.

Israel's Leadership Failure (vv. 1-16)

The account makes very clear why Joshua and his leaders failed. Verse 14 is explicit: they "did not ask for the counsel of the Lord." Until this instance, they had always sought guidance from the Lord through prayer. The question, therefore, is, why did they not ask counsel? And in its answer lies a volume of practical wisdom.

First, they did not ask counsel of the Lord because the Gibeonites looked authentic. They were a grubby crew! And in those days before regular bathing and deodorant, they even smelled authentic. Joshua and company did not seek God's counsel because the travelers *appeared* to be on the up and up.

Second, they did not seek counsel because things were going so well. They had let their guard down; they were confident and relaxed. Why should they be otherwise? The whole land was recoiling before them. This comes as no surprise. We are all prone to think ourselves independent of God as soon as things are going well. During trouble we pray continuously in great detail. But when everything is fine, it is hard even to think of what we should pray for.

The third reason Joshua did not go to the Lord for guidance was that this alliance with this little nation seemed "no big thing." Why bother God with the "little things?" Of course, such thinking is utterly fallacious! God calls us to take the so-called "small things" to Him as well as the greater. In fact, our taking the small things to Him often glorifies Him most, for it shows that we consider Him great enough to know and be interested in the insignificant things. And it is also a testing of our dependence upon Him.

In that moment when Joshua "did not ask counsel of the Lord," he was forgetting his very first recorded leadership lesson under Moses, when he saw the tide of battle against the Amalekites ebb and flow with the fall and rise of Moses' intercessory hands (Exodus 17:8-16). He forgot that prayer holds the greatest importance for spiritual leadership.

And Joshua's leadership failure had vast effects, for he brought an entire community of idolatrous Canaanites into Israel's midst! The danger was immense, for as Moses explained in Deuteronomy 7:2b, 4:

> You shall make no covenant with them and show no favor to them. . . . For they will turn your sons away from following Me to serve other gods; then the anger of the Lord will be kindled against you, and He will quickly destroy you.

The probability of idolatry and intermarriage was high, and God's sanctity was in danger of compromise—all because of this leadership lapse.

At this point we see a brilliant success for the forces of Satan. If ever the camel had its "nose in the tent," this was it! The Gibeonites' "Oscar-winning performance" had accomplished something which a frontal attack by all the united forces of the Canaanites could never have achieved. This "Gibeonite strategy" is, and always has been, a major trick in Satan's bag.

Jesus spoke of the same thing in the parable of the tares (Matthew 13:24-30), where tares sown by Satan in the wheat are so like the true grain that they are evident only by their fruit. Jesus says their roots so intertwine the real wheat that they cannot be separated until the harvest. And through the centuries, and today, the church still suffers through this insidious strategy, whether we refer to it as the peril of the tares or of the Gibeonites.

Effective spiritual leadership steels itself and its people against such assaults through prayer. Every decision must be taken before the Lord—even those we feel to be inconsequential. Before receiving another into alliance—whether it be a new church member, a spouse, or a business partner—we must ask counsel from the Lord! Think of the anguish the Body of Christ would be spared if this were the habit of its people. Never trust your judgment apart from Christ's counsel. If there is doubt, learn to wait. Proverbs 3:5-7, so often quoted, is perfect advice if taken to heart:

> Trust in the Lord with all your heart, and do not lean on your own understanding. In all your ways acknowledge Him, and He will make your paths straight. Do not be wise in your own eyes; fear the Lord and turn away from evil.

God's people faced serious danger because of the failure of their leadership to detect the Gibeonites' strategy. It was a fundamental error, because it involved the lack of prayer. What to do? Happily, verses 17-21 record the beautiful rebound of Israel's leadership.

Israel's Leadership Rebounds (vv. 17-21)

To begin with, Israel *keeps its word* and spares the Gibeonites, as verses 17 and 18 tell us:

> Then the sons of Israel set out and came to their cities on the third day. Now their cities were Gibeon and Chephirah and Beeroth and Kiriath-jearim. And the sons of Israel did not strike them because the leaders of the congregation had sworn to them by the Lord, the God of Israel.

Amazingly, the inhabitants of these four cities were spared any harm; not a hair of their Canaanite heads was touched. Israel's leadership held their people back—and that was not easy. The last part of verse 18 says, "And the whole congregation grumbled against the leaders." They evidently felt, and rightly so, that their leaders were breaking the rules given in Deuteronomy 7:2ff. But Israel's revived leadership stood staunch. Verse 19 says:

> But all the leaders said to the whole congregation, "We have sworn to them by the Lord, the God of Israel, and now we cannot touch them."

A holy people representing God must not lie. Because they bear His name, they must have a morality which honors Him.

Psalm 15:1 and 4 reads, "O Lord, who may abide in Thy tent? He who swears to his own hurt, and does not change." Calvin said of their refusal to break their word, "The sacred name of God is more precious than the wealth of a whole world."

This refusal to compromise initially caused confusion. The people fell to insecurity and distrust. The long-range effect, however, was a solid increase in credibility. The September 24, 1982 *Chicago Tribune* carried the story of the twin Moody Bible Institute students Kristen and Karen Turner, who returned a wallet containing $350. As they were returning to Moody about 9:00 P.M., they crossed Rush Street and, in the middle of the street, found a wallet. They picked it up, discovered $350 in it, and took it to the police station. That is an unusual thing in Chicago; so unusual, in fact, that it made the front page of the *Trib*. The *Trib's* story was that a man had gone out to test-drive a motorcycle and lost his wallet on Rush Street. When he got back and attempted to pay for the motorcycle, he discovered his loss. He mournfully told his friend that the money was gone and he would never find it unless the angels provided it. But two angels from Moody Bible Institute did! A story like this will do more than thousands of dollars' worth of publicity to enhance Moody's credibility in Chicago. And so it was with the leadership of Israel. Their refusal to give in to the pressure of the people, their commitment to principle, ultimately brought an increase in credibility.

Healthy spiritual leadership resists being stampeded by its failures. Strong leadership returns to principle after its failure and does not compound the wrong by impulsive action. Oh, that we would learn this well! Too many have compounded their errors by reflexively making decisions which took them to even lower depths. Here Joshua and his leaders stand tall again—and for all time.

Yet the problem of the Gibeonites remained. What to do? Surround them and make them captive cities? Deport them behind Israel's lines? Leave them alone? But who could trust them?

God, and Israel's Leadership Failure (vv. 22-27)

Though the text does not say it, Joshua surely sought the Lord's counsel, and this is what he did: he summoned the

Gibeonites and gave them a question and a curse. The question was: "Why have you deceived us, saying, 'We are very far from you,' when you are living within our land?" (v. 22). And the curse was, "Now therefore, you are cursed, and you shall never cease being slaves, both hewers of wood and drawers of water for the house of my God" (v. 23). And with that the Gibeonites from all four cities became humble servants to Israel.

The potential for corruption and perversion was immense; in the very heart of Israel lived the Gibeonites, hauling water and cutting wood for the Tabernacle. They were closer to the center of worship than any of Israel's tribes except the Levites. But amazingly, as Keil and Delitzsch have pointed out, there is no record anywhere that they "held out any inducement to Israel to join in idolatrous worship."[1] And here we must note that the Gibeonites were not without their virtues, for from the beginning they acknowledged that Israel had a transcendent God (see 9:9, 10, 24). Moreover, they came to share some qualities of Rahab, the fellow Canaanite and great woman of faith. Both Rahab and the Gibeonites believed that God was with the Israelites. Rahab told the Israelites:

> For we have heard how the Lord dried up the water of the Red Sea before you when you came out of Egypt, and what you did to the two kings of the Amorites who were beyond the Jordan, to Sihon and Og, whom you utterly destroyed. And when we heard it, our hearts melted and no courage remained in any man any longer because of you; for the Lord your God, He is God in heaven above and on earth beneath (2:10, 11).

Similarly, the Gibeonites said,

> Your servants have come from a very far country because of the fame of the Lord your God; for we have heard the report of Him and all that He did in Egypt, and all that He did to the two kings of the Amorites who were beyond the Jordan, to Sihon king of Heshbon and to Og king of Bashan who was at Ashtaroth (9:9, 10).

Rahab believed, though she lived in the midst of pagan Jericho. Her acknowledgment of Israel's transcendent God was utterly unique because her heathen gods were limited. She also used the Hebrew name Jehovah, which was God's high and holy name. The Gibeonites' testimony was not as exalted as Rahab's, but it is clear that they used the same name and glimpsed the same transcendence (cf. 9:9).

The parallels continue. Both the Gibeonites and Rahab were famous liars. Yet both proved their loyalty among God's people. Rahab hid the spies; the Gibeonites remained faithful to their oath. They never again sided with the Hivites, though they were of the same blood. Both willingly separated from their people. Rahab left the kingdom of God's enemies for the kingdom of His people. She left her king and culture. The Gibeonites left their confederacy and came over to God's people. Neither could be cast out from God's people—Rahab because of the spies' promise, and the Gibeonites because of the leaders' covenant. Both moved to the heart of Israel; Rahab as the ancestor of Christ, and the Gibeonites at the center of worship.

Subsequent history reveals that the Gibeonites stayed close to the altar of God. Though their job was servile at best, it ultimately led to a place of religious privilege. When the land was divided, Gibeon was one of the cities given to Aaron, and it became a special place of God. Four hundred years later David stored the Tabernacle at Gibeon (1 Chronicles 16:39; 21:29). At least one of King David's mighty men was a Gibeonite. And when David's son, Solomon, ascended the throne, he made burnt offerings at Gibeon. Furthermore, several hundred years later, when the Jews returned from captivity in the sixth century B.C., the list included Gibeonites. Finally, in the days of Nehemiah, Gibeonites are mentioned as being among the people who rebuilt the walls of Jerusalem (Nehemiah 3:7). How beautiful this all is! God used the sin of Israel, which allowed the Gibeonites entrance into their midst, to bring about the Gibeonites' inclusion in His people.

Hope for Failed Leadership

The story of Israel's leadership failure and the salvation of the Gibeonites, paradoxical as it is, gives us cause for optimism—for two reasons. One is that God preserved Israel in their spiritual failure. When Israel returned to principle, He used the inclusion of the Gibeonites (despite the terrible possibility of subversion) to be a blessing to all. And we all know that God often does the same thing today. The church is imperfect; there are tares among the people of God—people who say the same words, mouth the same doctrines, confess the same creed, but are not true believers. Sometimes they get in and cause trouble, but often it works out to be grace. Even in marriages where there has been a vast mistake, as the Apostle Paul says, sometimes God turns it to advantage. First Corinthians 7:13, 14 says:

> And a woman who has an unbelieving husband, and he consents to live with her, let her not send her husband away. For the unbelieving husband is sanctified through his wife, and the unbelieving wife is sanctified through her believing husband; for otherwise your children are unclean, but now they are holy.

So the story of the Gibeonites is fuel for hope. God often works good from the mistakes of His children.

The second reason for optimism comes from what the story of the Gibeonites tells us about our salvation. It tells us that, despite our sin and moral deficiencies, we may become a part of God's people. If the Gibeonites could be saved, so can we! They were liars and rebels, and so are we. If they could come without an invitation, how much greater is our assurance who have an open invitation. John tells us

> . . . that whoever believes may in Him have eternal life. For God so loved the world, that He gave His only begotten Son, that whoever believes in Him should not perish, but have eternal life (John 3:15, 16).

Jesus invites us, "Come to Me, all who are weary and heavy laden, and I will give you rest" (Matthew 11:28). These are His words to us Gibeonites.

Moreover, God will never break His oath to us! If the Gibeonites could rest on Israel's oath which was made under the Gibeonites' deception, how much more can we rest on God's oath to us? God will never break His word to us. What joy and hope this brings to life!

What hope this brings to those who are outside the grace of God. John said of Jesus: "But as many as received Him, to them He gave the right to become children of God, even to those who believe in His name" (John 1:12). Rahab fled her wicked city and found God. Gibeonites fled their wicked life and found new life. Have you fled your own wickedness? Have you taken up Christ's wonderful invitation?

Footnotes

1. C. F. Keil and F. Delitzsch, *Joshua, Judges and Ruth* (Grand Rapids: Eerdmans, 1963), p. 101.

11

"THE SUN STOOD STILL"
Joshua 10:1-43

Predictably, the Israelites' unfortunate covenant with the people of Gibeon brought a response from the surrounding Canaanite kings. They quickly formed a confederacy to fight against Gibeon, the traitor city. Verses 3-5 describe what happened:

> Therefore Adonizedek of Jerusalem sent word to Hoham king of Hebron and to Piram king of Jarmuth and to Japhia king of Lachish and to Debir king of Eglon, saying, "Come up to me and help me, and let us attack Gibeon, for it has made peace with Joshua and with the sons of Israel." So the five kings of the Amorites, the king of Jerusalem, the king of Hebron, the king of Jarmuth, and king of Lachish, and the king of Eglon, gathered together and went up, they with all their armies, and camped by Gibeon and fought against it.

Though at this point in the narrative Joshua did not yet know of the siege, his problems had greatly multiplied. Up to this time he had faced only individual cities—Jericho and Ai—but now a coalition of infuriated armies had emerged. And if this coalition succeeded in disciplining the Gibeonites (which appeared assured), the loose military confederacy would be galvanized into a tremendous fighting force. In the next hours Joshua was going to face an immense test of his recently questionable leadership. But this time, happily, he would achieve a glorious victory.

Joshua's conduct memorably demonstrated five ingredients necessary to win great battles. And because we are all immersed in spiritual warfare (Ephesians 6), his behavior provides us with indispensable wisdom about how we should fight our own battles for God.

The First Ingredient for Successful Warfare Involves a Commitment to Principle (vv. 6-9)

Verse 6 tells how the encircled Gibeonites sent a desperate last-minute plea to Joshua for help.

> Do not abandon your servants—come up to us quickly and save us and help us, for all the kings of the Amorites that live in the hill country have assembled against us.

How easy it would have been for Joshua to ignore this plea. In fact, he must have been greatly tempted to do so. Just a few days earlier, the Gibeonites had made him play the fool. His credibility as a leader had taken a nosedive. A less honorable man than Joshua might have rejoiced at the plea, for now he could get rid of the Gibeonites without any trouble to anyone.

But Joshua did not see it that way. Though his covenant with the Gibeonites did not specifically require mutual protection, his decision to make them servants did. So he upheld his duty to protect them, though he could easily have let it slide. Joshua did what was right; he stuck to principle even though it was inconvenient. He maintained perfect integrity—and in doing this he modeled a primary ingredient for fighting the battles of life.

Knowing that what you are doing is right, having a clear conscience, is an essential ingredient for doing battle. Joshua knew he was doing the right thing in defending the Gibeonites, and so he went in bounding confidence. In fact, as Joshua traveled to Gibeon's rescue, the Lord affirmed him,

> And the Lord said to Joshua, "Do not fear them, for I have given them into your hands; not one of them shall stand before you"(v. 8).

Many of us have experienced the same thing. No matter how difficult the challenge may be, if we know we are doing the right thing, if our consciences are clear, we find ourselves vastly more competent to face the trial. On the other hand, if some of us are tentative and unsteady in the battles we face, it may be because we doubt that we are doing what is right—or because our hearts are not right. If this is the case, we need to retrench and seek the Lord's direction, examining our lives in the light of His Word. Proverbs 11:3 says, "The integrity of the upright will guide them."

Joshua led his men on a twenty-mile forced march up three thousand feet in the dark, armed with the first ingredient for successful battle—the knowledge in their heart of hearts that they were doing the right thing.

The Second Ingredient for Successful Warfare Involves Help from God (vv. 10, 11)

Verses 9 and 10 describe Joshua's surprise attack:

> So Joshua came upon them suddenly by marching all night from Gilgal. And the Lord confounded them before Israel, and He slew them with a great slaughter at Gibeon, and pursued them by the way of the ascent of Beth-horon and struck them as far as Azekah and Makkedah.

Joshua had them on the run, and then God intervened in a stupendous way:

> And it came about as they fled from before Israel, while they were at the descent of Beth-horon, that the Lord threw large stones from heaven on them as far as Azekah, and they died; there were more who died from hailstones than those whom the sons of Israel killed with the sword (v. 11).

The fleeing armies had begun to outdistance the foot-weary army of Israel, who were exhausted by their all-night march; so the Lord opened up with the artillery of heaven.

No one could miss the significance of this great storm: God was fighting for Israel. His people were supposed to constantly keep this realization before them when they fought their wars. In fact, Deuteronomy 20:3, 4 commands that whenever Israel arrayed itself for battle, a priest should come near and say,

> Hear, O Israel, you are approaching the battle against your enemies today. Do not be fainthearted. Do not be afraid, or

> panic, or tremble before them, for the Lord your God is the one who goes with you, to fight for you against your enemies, to save you.

Joshua's dramatic nighttime encounter with a mystic warrior brandishing a sword taught them the same things (5:13-15). The "captain of the host" (a theophany) was saying, "I am going to fight your battles with you." Thus, when we fight, we must understand, as Joshua did, that God fights with us and for us.

Here the hailstones teach us that we will never succeed in battle without God's help, no matter how capable and well-armed we are. In fact, we have never won a battle in which God has not fought for us. This is the conclusion we must reach if we honestly read the sixth chapter of Ephesians. Each of the pieces of armor we are commanded to wear—the belt of truth, the breastplate of righteousness, the gospel shoes, the shield of faith, and the helmet of salvation—demonstrates that it is God who gives us energy for our battles. Behind each of those pieces of armor is a dimension of God's power. So we, like Joshua, fight in utter dependence on God. This dependence anticipates the third ingredient of successful warfare.

The Third Ingredient of Successful Warfare Involves an Effective Prayer Life (vv. 12-14)

And here Joshua offers a prayer *par excellence*. There has never been anything like it!

> Then Joshua spoke to the Lord in the day when the Lord delivered up the Amorites before the son of Israel, "O sun, stand still at Gibeon, and O moon in the valley of Aijalon." So the sun stood still, and the moon stopped, until the nation avenged themselves of their enemies. Is it not written in the Book of Jashar? And the sun stopped in the middle of the sky, and did not hasten to go down for about a whole day. And there was no day like that before it or after it, when the Lord listened to the voice of a man; for the Lord fought for Israel. Then Joshua and all Israel with him returned to the camp to Gilgal (vv. 12-15).

When you can order the sun and the moon to stand still, you've got it together!

There have been a number of theories about what really happened on that day. Some are not acceptable, such as the one that insists this is simply poetic imagery describing how the sun, in the heat of battle, *seemed* to stand still. Neither is the view acceptable which says that the Hebrew really means "the sun and moon ceased to shine." This interpretation simply does not hold up linguistically, as such scholars as John Bright, G. Ernest Wright, and John Davis have shown.[1]

The only acceptable view is that God extended daylight for a full day over the battle area. Some believe that this happened because the earth's rotation slowed. Others believe God did it by tilting the earth so that daylight was extended, much as it is near the North Pole where, at certain times of the year, the sun does not set. Still others argue that the miracle was localized due to a refraction of the sun's rays, such as might occur with the Northern Lights.[2]

In my opinion any one of these three explanations could be true—or perhaps some other. If we are concerned about the obvious physical complications of tilting the earth or slowing it down, we must remember that if God is pleased to modify the speed or tilt of the earth or the refraction of light, He will also be able to adjust all relative phenomena, and then make all things run together harmoniously. The important thing is that it happened—and that it happened in response to Joshua's prayer. So powerful was Joshua's prayer that the Scripture says, "there was no day like that before it or after it, when the Lord listened to the voice of a man" (v. 14).

Prayer is an indispensable ingredient to getting the job done—winning the battles of our lives. When my son Kent was in nursery school, we discovered that he had multiple learning disabilities. This became clear after he had surgery to correct a wandering eye, which the doctor thought was at the root of the problem. His difficulties were so complicated that in the fifth grade he could normally repeat back three nonsequential numbers or words like "seven, five, eight," but if another was added, it was nearly impossible. This made memorization out of the question. I remember a Christmas play in which Kent played a Wise Man and had only one line. He worked on memorizing it with us during an eight hundred mile car trip, but could not get it right. On the night of the play, however, he did. I'll never forget the moment he stood with the other shepherds in costume wearing his black tennies, his eyes wide with tension.

Strange feelings come upon me
  Though I know not why
The night is still around me,
  The stars shine in the sky.

How proud we were!

A long succession of doctors, tests, and consultations revealed that he was quite intelligent, but both his audio and visual perceptual faculties were impaired. This meant that he had to work many times harder than his sisters and brother to assimilate the same information. And he has! As he went on to junior high and high school, every course required seemingly endless hours of hard, hard work. His education has been a painful experience. There are very few days in the last fourteen years that my wife, Barbara, and I have not prayed for Kent in this respect. We have prayed more for his success in school than for anything else in our lives. And Kent has done it!

When Kent graduated from high school, we invited our pastoral staff to his graduation ceremony. We also had all the extended family, relatives, and friends there. We armed them with streamers and confetti. As Kent walked across the platform to receive his diploma, we thundered in unison, "Way to go, Kent!" and showered the sedate audience with confetti and streamers. They loved it! And Kent? He flashed a big smile because he knew it was his day of victory. It was our day of victory, too—and one of the great days of our lives. We can truly say that there was "no day like it before." Why? Because "the Lord listened to the voice of a man." He heard Kent's prayers and ours.

Prayer is the indispensable ingredient for meeting and winning the great battles of life. Joshua knew it. He had a vital prayer life. We know it is true, too. What are the ingredients for getting the job done for Christ? First, doing what is right; second, acknowledging help from God; and third, having an effective prayer life.

The Fourth Ingredient for Successful Warfare Involves a Willingness to Do the Job Yourself (vv. 12-14)

If we read Joshua's prayer carefully, we note that he does not ask for God to do it; rather, Joshua asks for *more time* to get the job done. "Stand still, sun and moon, and I'll do the job myself." After all, he could have asked for more hailstones. Why not? God had already demonstrated His willingness to use them when unsolicited. Very possibly, if Joshua were a modern man, he would have asked God to do the whole thing. Why get one's hands dirty when someone else can do the job?

We must understand that God is interested in the *process* that brings victory, perhaps as much as in the victory itself. The Israelites' participation in the battle made the land theirs. They had invested their lives in obtaining it. They had won it. They owned it. If they had not participated in the battle, if God had simply provided a victory, they would not have held the conquest so dear.

When we face great problems, our prayers should include a willingness to be part of the answer. We must stand ready to wrestle the problem through and grow with the process. Have you been praying that God would deliver you from some difficulty? Or praying for an easy way out? Perhaps you need to change your prayer and say, "God, I will do the job if You want me to. Just give me the courage and the time."

The Fifth Ingredient for Successful Warfare Involves Confidence (v. 25)

The fifth and final ingredient for success in life's battles is confidence in God. Verses 16-43 record Joshua's systematic subjugation of the five kings and the remaining cities in southern Palestine. During all of this Joshua remained supremely confident. God's words at the onset still rang in his ears: "Do not fear them, for I have given them into your hand; not one of them shall stand before you." Joshua believed this, and his confidence overflowed to others. Verses 24 and 25 tell us:

> And it came about when they brought these kings out to Joshua, that Joshua called for all the men of Israel, and said to the chiefs of the men of war who had gone with him, "Come

> near, put your feet on the necks of these kings." So they came near and put their feet on their necks. Joshua then said to them, "Do not fear or be dismayed! Be strong and courageous, for thus the Lord will do to all your enemies with whom you fight."

Joshua's words are for us. The Lord will defeat our enemies. He will conquer our problems. God is faithful! The Lord says to His people, "For I know the plans that I have for you . . . plans for welfare and not for calamity to give you a future and a hope" (Jeremiah 29:11). At the end of the first chapter of Philippians, beautiful verse 28 says: ". . . [stand] in no way alarmed by your opponents—which is a sign of destruction for them, but of salvation for you." When they see your confidence, when they see you really believe, you are on your way to victory.

The second and greater Joshua was the Lord Jesus Christ. Jesus bore Joshua's name ("Jehovah is salvation") because He is the Captain of our salvation, and He wrought a far greater victory than the first Joshua. Moreover, Jesus more perfectly modeled all the *ingredients* of successful spiritual warfare than the original Joshua.

> Jesus was always committed to principle, to doing what was right. He said, "I always do the will of Him who sent Me." This assurance gave Him the fortitude to fight the greatest battle ever fought.
>
> Jesus always depended upon God the Father. We see His dependence when he constantly speaks to God as "Abba"—"Dearest Father." His dependence wrought the resurrection.
>
> Jesus was always in prayer, and the Father heard His words. Jesus was willing to do the job Himself; that is what the Incarnation means. He was willing to come in contact with the sinful world to save it. He did not take the easy way.
>
> Finally, Jesus was perfectly confident in God. He always knew He would win. He always knew that every knee would bow before Him.

We should realize that all the ingredients that would take us on to victory, were perfected in Christ; and by virtue of the

Holy Spirit and our incorporation into Christ, we can now have these ingredients. Armed and armored, as Jesus was, with integrity, prayer, willingness to face challenges, and confidence in the Father, we cannot fail.

Footnotes

1. John Bright, *The Interpreter's Bible,* Vol. 2 (Nashville: Abingdon, 1953), p. 605; Robert G. Boling and G. Ernest Wright, *Joshua,* The American Bible Series (New York: Doubleday, 1982); John J. Davis, *Conquest and Crisis: Studies in Joshua, Judges and Ruth* (Grand Rapids: Baker, 1976).
2. Davis (pp. 67-69) provides a simple, lucid explanation of this view.

12

CALEB: GREEN AND GROWING
Joshua 14:1-15

In the middle of chapter 10 of Joshua, after Israel's victory over the southern confederation of kings at Gibeon, the content abruptly changes from dramatic narrative to a tedious recitation of the names of the cities conquered and the areas given to each of the tribes of Israel. This list continues for another eleven chapters before the story returns to its more active pace in chapter 22.* Thus, chapters 11 through 21 provide very little opportunity for practical application—with a few bright exceptions. The first of these exceptions comes in chapter 14, with the story of Caleb's inheritance.

Caleb at this time was well past "retirement age." He was an octogenarian, eighty-five years old. His age and what he did are what make this chapter so significant and bright, for Caleb did not conform to the twentieth-century stereotype of old age. None of us would argue the fact that old age brings change. Our experience attests to that. You know, for instance, that you are aging when you go to a wedding and the mother of the bride looks better to you than the bride! Age does bring change. But if we think that age necessarily brings weakness and ineffectiveness, we are sorely wrong. Caleb's example teaches us that old age can be a time of great power—even a time of maximum influence and usefulness.

Why is it that Caleb was so effective in old age? The answer provides insight for all of us, no matter what age. If the little gray-haired lady who helped you across the street is your wife, this is for you. If you are young, this is for you, too, because you are going to be there sooner than you think—and you might as well get there in the right way.

*See the Appendix for an outline of chapters 10 through 20.

A Life of Faith

The primary reason for Caleb's effectiveness in his later years is that he led a life full of faith. He burst into the pages of Holy Scripture, in fact, with a supreme demonstration of that faith. The thirteenth chapter of Numbers tells us that Moses, on the verge of crossing the Jordan and entering the Promised Land, commissioned twelve spies—one from each of Israel's tribes—to scout out the land; Caleb was selected from the tribe of Judah, along with Hoshea (that is, Joshua) from the tribe of Ephraim (cf. Numbers 13:6-8). The spy party found a remarkably fertile land crowded with people, for it lay across the great highways of trade and travel in the ancient world. It was a wonderful land—upon this they all agreed. They differed, however, on Israel's chances of possessing Canaan.

The majority report from ten of the spies came completely from the human viewpoint—from ground level. They stated their conclusion in regrettably memorable terms.

> So they gave out to the sons of Israel a bad report of the land which they had spied out, saying, "The land through which we have gone, in spying it out, is a land that devours its inhabitants; and all the people whom we saw in it are men of great size. There also we saw the Nephilim (the sons of Anak are part of the Nephilim); and we became like grasshoppers in our own sight, and so we were in their sight" (Numbers 13:32, 33).

Their perspective was totally *ad hominem*. God did not figure in their thinking—and their grasshopper complex. On the other hand, the minority report stated the divine perspective. Here it appears that Caleb took the lead in quieting the people and calling them to arms (Numbers 13:30). Together Caleb and Joshua said taking Canaan would be like eating bread—"a piece of cake" (Numbers 14:9). Caleb's faith was alive and virile! The Anakim did not intimidate him. Certainly they were big; but from above, from the divine perspective, they were just dots on the earth. Caleb's faith said, "Go for it!"

God's Promises to Caleb

Because Caleb trusted God's power, the Lord gave him two promises through the lips of Moses. Though Numbers does not record them, verses 9 and 10 of Joshua 14 do. The first promise was the land of Hebron:

> So Moses swore on that day, saying, "Surely the land on which your foot has trodden shall be an inheritance for you and to your children forever, because you have followed the Lord my God fully" (v. 9).

Evidently, of the twelve spies, only Caleb had the courage to set foot in Hebron where the Anakim dwelt. The others skirted the area, but he bravely infiltrated it. Caleb scouted out the area, walked among these people, and returned. Therefore God said, through Moses, "You are going to have that land because you set your feet to it by faith."

Secondly, God promised Caleb longevity, for he says,

> And now behold, the Lord has let me live, just as He spoke, these forty-five years, from the time that the Lord spoke this word to Moses, when Israel walked in the wilderness; and now behold, I am eighty-five years old today (v. 10).

The point is, Caleb not only exhibited great faith through his belief that Israel could take the land; he also continued to demonstrate faith by believing God's promises that he would live long and possess his part of the land. This faith becomes particularly remarkable against the dark background of Israel's pervasive unbelief. Caleb believed when others' faith failed. Moreover, he kept on believing for forty-five long years.

Three times Joshua 14 describes Caleb's faith with the assertion that he "followed the Lord fully." In verse 8 he says it of himself: "my brethren who went up with me made the heart of the people melt with fear; but I followed the Lord my God fully." In verse 9 Moses is quoted as saying it of him. And in verse 14 Joshua says,

> Therefore Hebron became the inheritance of Caleb the son of Jephunneh the Kenizzite until this day, because he followed the Lord God of Israel fully.

What a sublime compliment. He saw his people drop away, one by one, until all who had come out of Egypt lay in desert graves. He saw Moses climb to his lonely grave and heard his farewell. And still Caleb "followed the Lord God of Israel fully." He took God's promises and personalized them. They were his own.

Aged Caleb had an amazingly effective "postretirement" because his life was one of faith. We draw from this the truth: *those who base their lives on God's promises, "following the Lord fully," will find themselves effective in old age.* We, too, need to cultivate our faith now if we want the future years to be what they should be. The more one exercises faith, the easier it comes. Conversely, if faith has not been a part of one's life, it comes harder with the years. According to the Bible, the greatest years of faith and effectiveness ought to be the later years. We should have greater faith, and thereby greater effectiveness, at twenty than fifteen; and then it should increase in the thirties, the forties, the fifties, and the sixties. We ought to be greater believers at eighty! I personally believe that if my heart grows in faith and dedication, if I become more and more a man of the Word, then my very best work for the Lord may well come when I am eighty—if I live that long.

A Youthful Life

Caleb was effective in old age because of his faith. He was also effective because he led a youthful life. Verses 10 and 11 record that Caleb says of himself:

> And now behold, the Lord has let me live, just as He spoke, these forty-five years, from the time that the Lord spoke this word to Moses, when Israel walked in the wilderness; and now behold, I am eighty-five years old today. I am still as strong today as I was in the day Moses sent me; as my strength was then, so my strength is now, for war and for going out and coming in.

Why was Caleb so strong? The first answer has to be divine enablement. God gave him a strong body and longevity. But here we must make sure we do not consider longevity and a healthy body the predictable result of a good life. Many have been born with weakened bodies and constitutions. Moreover, it is not God's will for everyone to live to eighty-five or ninety. Youthful strength is not so much the emphasis here as a youthful spirit. Caleb's secret was his devotion to God.

The secret of a perpetual spirit of youth and strength lies in giving ourselves to God and living for Him. We all know that a godly life is instrinsically a healthy life because it encourages good health habits, but that is not what we have in view here. Rather, Caleb exemplifies a godly attitude—the optimism, growing interests, and broadening sympathies that come with a life of devotion. Such a life is not a matter of age. Some men and women in their thirties are old—aged in spirit. If your only ambition is simply to make money and be comfortable, you are old right now.

On the other hand, some people stay young, even grow younger, with the years. Such was the life of College Church's (Wheaton, Illinois) beloved pastor Evan Welsh. Pastor Welsh held the pulpit of College Church from 1933 to 1946, went to Ward Memorial Presbyterian Church in Detroit, and then returned to Wheaton College to serve as Chaplain and Alumni Chaplain. If ever there was a man with a young heart, he was the man. He kept a young man's pace. He had a young man's optimism. He would tackle anyone and any situation. Why? Because of his devotion to the Lord. Psalm 92:12-14 was fulfilled in his life:

> The righteous man will flourish like the palm tree,
> He will grow a cedar in Lebanon.
> Planted in the house of the Lord,
> They will flourish in the courts of our God.
> They will still yield fruit in old age;
> They shall be full of sap and very green.

Evan Welsh was green and growing until the day he died. And so was Caleb.

The one motivation that never wears out is serving the Lord. With age, many natural motivations may begin to weaken, such as the desire for personal success or fame or the natural appetites of the flesh. But the one motivation that never slackens for the devoted heart is service to God. This was Paul's experience, which he so beautifully stated in 2 Corinthians 4:16: "Therefore we do not lose heart, but though our outer man is decaying, yet our inner man is being renewed day by day." Surely Caleb experienced this too. And his lively spirit, his perpetual youth, led him to do great things for God. Serious Christianity brings a completely positive outlook to aging. The day came when Stan Smith, the great tennis player, was regularly being beaten by some of the newcomers on the tour, and someone asked him about it. He took a couple of tennis balls, one very old and flat and the other new. He dropped them both. One bounced and bounced, and the other bounced just a few times. Smith said, "That's the difference." "The outer man is decaying," becoming wrinkled and old, but "the inner man is being renewed day by day." What a way to go. How perpetually positive this makes us.

Why was Caleb so effective in old age? First, because he led a life of faith. Second, because he had a youthful spirit which was a by-product of his devotion. And, finally, he led a life of faith because he eagerly faced new and trying situations for the Lord.

A Life Which Welcomes Challenge

At eighty-five Caleb was ready for another battle. These are his words of challenge:

> I am still as strong today as I was in the day Moses sent me; as my strength was then, so my strength is now, for war and for going out and coming in. Now then, give me this hill country about which the Lord spoke on that day, for you heard on that day that Anakim were there, with great fortified cities; perhaps the Lord will be with me, and I shall drive them out as the Lord has spoken.

A fire had been smoldering in his heart for forty-five years; now, when he saw the land, it flamed again. Caleb's words, "perhaps the Lord will be with me," were words neither of faltering faith nor ironic bravado. He simply meant that if it was God's will to do it through him, it would be done.

Caleb knew what he was in for. He had seen the walled cities of Hebron and the Anakim. But he went for it.

> Now he gave to Caleb the son of Jephunneh a portion among the sons of Judah, according to the command of the Lord to Joshua, namely, Kiriath-arba, Arba being the father of Anak (that is, Hebron). And Caleb drove out from there

> the three sons of Anak: Sheshai and Ahiman and Talmai, the children of Anak. Then he went up from there against the inhabitants of Debir; now the name of Debir formerly was Kiriath-sepher (15:13-15).

What a man this Caleb was!

Such vigor is not typical of old age. The natural tendency is to seek comfort and a life away from the fray. Old age, many think, is a time to withdraw and consider oneself—a time to leave the battles to the younger—a time for deserved rest. What a beautiful thing it is when we see those who think otherwise.

What about some of us today? What about you who are reaching retirement age, the years when you will have some time? Do you realize that Moses began his career at eighty? Winston Churchill still spoke powerfully when he approached his eighties. Michelangelo completed his greatest painting, "The Fresco of the Last Judgment" in the Sistine Chapel, when he was almost seventy. What about those of you in mid-life? Thinking about IRAs and tax shelters, and dreaming of a time when you don't have to do anything? Maybe we need to begin dreaming of a life like Caleb's—green in old age, still "going for it!"

Finally, note that Caleb's effectiveness and devotion made his long life rich, full, and satisfying. It is a fact that the remainder of Israel never achieved the fulfillment God had for them. They never fully took what He promised. When Joshua was old, despite his victories, there was still much land to possess.

> Now Joshua was old and advanced in years when the Lord said to him, "You are old and advanced in years, and very much of the land remains to be possessed" (13:1).

Though Israel had broken the backbone of the enemy, much mopping up remained. And the Lord had promised to help His people do it:

> All the inhabitants of the hill country from Lebanon as far as Misrephoth-maim, all the Sidonians, I will drive them out from before the sons of Israel; only allot it to Israel for an inheritance as I have commanded you (13:6).

In other words: "Go ahead, divide the land—because I'm going to give you the strength to clear it up and possess what I've set aside for you." But Israel failed miserably. Why did they not take what belonged to them? Joshua 17:13 gives the answer:

> And it came about when the sons of Israel became strong, they put the Canaanites to forced labor, but they did not drive them out completely.

They failed because the enemy was difficult to root out; it seemed much easier to make them slaves and draw tribute from them. Israel failed because they preferred peace and prosperity to the full blessings and possessions of God.

Caleb, on the other hand, experienced complete possession and fulfillment. He refused to fall prey to the "peace and prosperity" syndrome; instead, he went for it all. Hastings says of him:

> Of all the Israelites who received their inheritance in the Land of Promise, Caleb appears to have been the only one who succeeded in entirely expelling the native occupiers of the country. The Israelites generally seem to have made but poor headway against their strong and mighty foes, with their chariots of iron and fenced walls. Repeatedly we encounter the sorrowful affirmation that they were not able to drive them out. But Caleb was a notable exception. What though Arba was the greatest man among the Anakim (Joshua 14:15), what though his three grandsons, Sheshai, and Ahiman, and Talmai, the sons of Anak, were prepared to yield their lives rather than give up possession (15:14), Caleb drove them out—not he indeed, but the Lord, who was with him, and gave him a victory that must have otherwise eluded even his strong hands. The man who "wholly followed the Lord" was alone wholly victorious.[1]

If you and I are Christians, the main battle has been won—just as Israel's southern and northern campaigns broke the heart of the enemy's resistance. But it still remains for us to take our possessions. God has given us the power to defeat our enemies by assailing their castles dark. Jesus has lost none of His power since saving us. But we must use it. The great challenge is that we, like Caleb of old, must resist the allurement of peace and prosperity which drove Israel into making a treaty with the enemy. We all desire to find a comfortable place away from the fray. We would all like to be at peace with the culture around us. But this can never be for the committed heart, the Caleb heart.

As we grow older, may we resist the pull of comfort and peace and pursue a life of effectiveness. Let us live first a life of faith, "following the Lord fully" in all that we do. If we do this, we will find old age to be rich and full. Second, let us pursue a youthful spirit—the kind of spirit that comes from commitment to Him, a spirit that intensifies with age, one of perpetual youth. Third, let us live life with a spirit that welcomes challenge, for such a spirit never grows old. Let us say with Caleb,

> Now then, give me this hill country about which the Lord spoke on that day, for you heard on that day that Anakim were there, with great fortified cities; perhaps the Lord will be with me, and I shall drive them out as the Lord has spoken (14:12).

If God is saying to you, "I want you to have an effective life," then grab onto Caleb's life. Allow him to take you by the hand and draw you up with him so that you will have a perpetual youthful spirit and a willingness to face new challenges, not looking for "Saints' Rest," not looking for peace and comfort. Follow him and you will be effective, even at the end of life.

Footnotes

1. James Hastings, ed., *The Great Men and Women of the Bible, Moses—Samson,* Vol. II (Edinburgh: T & T Clark, 1914), p. 422.

13

KEEPING *SHALOM* IN ISRAEL
Joshua 22:1-34

At a time when most people romanticized our country's Civil War, Stephen Crane dispelled its mythic drama and glory. In his great work *The Red Badge of Courage,* Crane portrayed the reality of war—its naked terrors, its misery, its contradictions, ambivalences, and ironies. His picture of the young soldier, wounded, wandering deliriously with the other injured behind his own lines, is unforgettable.

War has always been a miserable affair. It was the same for the Israelites in their day, even though they had won. Their seven-year campaign for possession of Palestine had given them enough hunger, exposure, forced marches, blood, and exhaustion to last a lifetime. When peace came, they were ready!

Joshua 21:43-45 capsulizes the outcome of war for the *Bene Israel,* the sons of Israel:

> So the Lord gave Israel all the land which He had sworn to give to their fathers, and they possessed it and lived in it. And the Lord gave them rest on every side, according to all that He had sworn to their fathers, and no one of all their enemies stood before them; the Lord gave all their enemies into their hand. Not one of the good promises which the Lord had made to the house of Israel failed; all came to pass.

The nine and a half tribes which made up the bulk of Israel had attained their peace. Every good promise was fulfilled as they took their allotted portions of the Promised Land. This new existence, this state of *shalom,* included not only the absence of war, but everything that made for a full, complete life. It was wonderful.

Shalom and inheritance were also given to the two and one-half tribes (the tribes of Reuben, Gad, and the half-tribe of Manasseh) to whom God had promised land on the other side of the Jordan. As you may remember, when Joshua began the campaign for Palestine, he allowed the women, children, livestock, and shepherds of the two and one-half tribes to remain on the other side of the Jordan, but he commanded that their warriors help their brothers in the nine and one-half other tribes conquer the Promised Land. So they willingly sent forty thousand armed men in the van of Israel (cf. 1:12-16 and 4:11-13). Now, in giving them their inheritance, Joshua complimented them. No doubt his words were drawn with emotion:

> Then Joshua summoned the Reubenites and the Gadites and the half-tribe of Manasseh, and said to them, "You have kept all that Moses the servant of the Lord commanded you, and have listened to my voice in all that I commanded you. You have not forsaken your brothers these many days to this day, but have kept the charge of the commandment of the Lord your God. And now the Lord your God has given rest to your brothers, as He spoke to them; therefore, turn now and go to your tents, to the land of your possession, which Moses the servant of the Lord gave you beyond the Jordan" (vv. 1-4).

Joshua was very complimentary, very generous in his praise—and well he should have been, for those who remained of the forty thousand soldiers had given seven years, away from their families and land, to help their brothers secure their inheritance. Joshua held these faithful men dear. And as they prepared to cross back over the Jordan, he felt much like a parent who watches a child go away to school or out into the world. His concern was that they keep the faith. He realized that the Jordan and its difficult geography would make a formidable challenge to their unity, both political and spiritual. No doubt some wary variation of "out of sight, out of mind" coursed through his thinking.

He thus charged them to the deepest spiritual commitment

with six short commands. And here his voice must have swelled with even greater emotion:

> "Only be very careful to observe the commandment and the law which Moses the servant of the Lord commanded you, to love the Lord your God and walk in all His ways, and keep His commandments and hold fast to Him and serve Him with all your heart and with all your soul." So Joshua blessed them and sent them away, and they went to their tents (vv. 5, 6).

Joshua charged them to guard their hearts. He knew that if they stayed focused on God, and if the rest of Israel also did so, they would keep their blessed unity. Joshua's concern was valid. Would Israel remain one? Distance and time would certainly work against it. Was there more to this good-bye than appeared?

The Scriptural writer records their departure in verse 9, but he does not tell the half of it. He only gives the barest facts, like the back page of *The Wall Street Journal:*

> And the sons of Reuben and the sons of Gad and the half-tribe of Manasseh returned home and departed from the sons of Israel at Shiloh which is in the land of Canaan, to go to the land of Gilead, to the land of their possession which they had possessed, according to the command of the Lord through Moses (v. 9).

The real story is this: the men of the two and one-half tribes strode throughout the great camp of Israel, singling out their dearest brothers, and, with tears, embraced them. The blood of war had bound them together. "There is a comradeship among men in titanic moments that is one of the great mystiques of life."[1] Poignant, masculine Middle-Eastern good-byes filled the air. There were few dry eyes. Their blood had been mixed in battle and their swords had rung side by side, so they embraced each other and wept on each other's shoulders.

This parting caused immense pain for the sons of Israel because of the profound exchange which had taken place between them as they fought together. But now they had separated. Peace, *shalom,* and rest were with all of God's people on both sides of the Jordan. Would it stay that way? Were Joshua's concerns valid? The answers came sooner than any could have expected—and they were not good.

Israel's Peace and Rest Threatened (vv. 10-12)

Immediately their newly-departed comrades built a huge altar, right next to the Jordan, which looked just like the great altar at Shiloh. Apparently it was a rival to the authorized original. Verses 10-12 describe the events:

> And when they came to the region of the Jordan which is in the land of Canaan, the sons of Reuben and the sons of Gad and the half-tribe of Manasseh built an altar there by the Jordan, a large altar in appearance. And the sons of Israel heard it saying, "Behold, the sons of Reuben and the sons of Gad and the half-tribe of Manasseh have built an altar at the frontier of the land of Canaan, in the region of the Jordan, on the side belonging to the sons of Israel." And when the sons of Israel heard of it, the whole congregation of the sons of Israel gathered themselves at Shiloh, to go up against them in war.

It was bold apostasy! How could it have happened so soon? They could not believe their eyes, but there stood the evidence. All the men of faithful Israel girded on their worn scabbards and armor. Unbelievably, they were now going to fight their former comrades-in-arms.

Was Israel right or wrong here? As so often happens in life, they were both right *and* wrong. They were right in that, though they had had more than enough of fighting, they were willing to go to war again to avert apostasy. Many of them must have wept. But they had no choice. "We cannot allow the honor of God to be compromised, though we are sick of war." They believed that there was something more important than their own lives—namely, the holiness of God (cf. Deuteronomy 13:13, 15, 16 and Leviticus 17:8, 9).

Israel's attitude provides a healthy, refreshing contrast to the contemporary mind-set, which insists that such issues should provoke neither conflict nor argument. "God, truth, virtue—about these things honorable men and women disagree. Civilized people don't get worked up about these," says the urbane modern. But just touch anything that affects his material well-being and there is war.

We must applaud Israel for her willingness to die for God's name. His people had the right idea. But they were also wrong, because they immediately jumped to the worst possible conclusion about their ex-comrades. Most people, unfortunately, are negative by nature. When R. H. Fulton tested his steamboat, people stood on the shore and chanted, "It will never start, never start, never start." And then, when it started and began to move, they changed their chant to, "It will never stop, never stop, never stop." Spiritually, we have a sad tendency to believe the worst of others, a disposition to gloat over a discovered fault, a habit of cultivating a suspicious spirit which we vainly imagine is wisdom.

The Scriptures enjoin us to be different. Paul says love "believes all things, hopes all things" (1 Corinthians 13:7). We are to believe the best about others until we have no other alternative. We ought never to rush to the worst interpretation. If we all trusted our fellow-believers like this, the church of Christ would be spared much of its misery.

As the situation stood, tragedy loomed. For Israel to crush one-third of her people would have cost the lives of another third, and then the survivors would have been at the mercy of the Canaanites. Fortunately, some cooler heads prevailed and what they did maintained the precious peace and unity of God's people. What happens here in Joshua 22 is not just history. For God's people today, it is an example of how we should daily deal with one another. It is an example for all times.

Israel's Rest and Peace Preserved and Perpetuated (vv. 13-34)

How did Israel preserve its rest and peace? *Shalom* was saved first by the model action of the larger body of Israel, and then by the model response of the nation's offending smaller part. After the bad start, Israel modeled the four-step proper approach to this problem.

First, according to verses 13 and 14, they formed an investigative committee of spiritual leaders. The committee was made up of Phinehas, the son of Eleazar, the high priest, and one leader from each of the ten tribes in Palestine. No doubt, in the emotion of the moment, some others opposed forming this committee, saying, "There's no need to investigate. It's ridiculous. Why else would the two and one-half tribes build an altar but to establish their own worship? I say we attack before they become entrenched. We can't allow this blasphemy to go on another minute." But the responsible leadership of Israel did not give in—and the committee crossed over the Jordan to find out the truth. Thus, they took the first positive step by forming an in-depth investigative committee.

Second, as verse 15 tells us, they went directly to the offenders and talked with them face to face. "And they came to the sons of Reuben and to the sons of Gad and to the half-tribe of Manasseh, to the land of Gilead, and they spoke with them." From my perspective as a pastor and observer of the human situation, this is a courageous approach. People typically deal with suspected sinners by talking to everyone else *but* them. Why? Because the suspicious spirit which readily believes the worst about another is generally wedded to a cowardice which does not dare ask if its conclusions are right. How many friendships have been ruined, how much lifelong misery created by the lack of courage to go to a friend and ask an explanation? We must never let the fear of being thought unloving permit us to be unloving. We must be like Israel, which brought the charges to the offenders in person.

The third appropriate action Israel took was this: they were explicit in expressing their concerns to their brothers. They didn't "beat around the bush," as verse 16 clearly demonstrates:

> Thus says the whole congregation of the Lord, "What is this unfaithful act which you have committed against the God of Israel, turning away from following the Lord this day, by building yourselves an altar, to rebel against the Lord this day?"

They spoke with commendable candor and frankness. Verses 17, 18, and 20 reveal that they also let their brothers know that they themselves feared being judged by God for their brothers' sin, because they were all one people in spiritual solidarity. That, after all, was what had happened in the case of the sin at Baal-Peor (vv. 17, 18) and with Achan (v. 20). The whole nation had suffered for the sin of the few, and they did not want it to happen again. Here their understanding foreshadowed the New Testament teaching, "if one member suffers, all suffer for it" (1 Corinthians 12:26); "for not one of us lives for himself, and not one dies for himself" (Romans 17:7). This appeal on the basis of spiritual solidarity must have stirred all their hearts.

Finally, verse 29 tells us that they showed magnanimity in the midst of making their accusation:

> If, however, the land of your possession is unclean then cross into the land of the possession of the Lord, where the Lord's tabernacle stands, and take possession among us. Only do not rebel against the Lord, or rebel against us by building an altar for yourselves, besides the altar of the Lord our God (v. 19).

They laced their accusation with remarkable love and generosity. "Listen, our brothers, if you don't want to remain on the other side of the Jordan, if you feel that you cannot be blessed over there, then return here. We'll make room for you. We'll vacate enough villages. We'll give you our land. But please do not begin a rival, unlawful religion, as you are doing with this altar." Unlawful sacrifice would have cost the majority of Israel greatly. It would have negatively affected their material well-being. This was a beautiful offer. And, quite naturally, it had a calming effect on those stung by the barbs of accusation.

As we shall see, greater Israel's care in forming an investigative committee, her direct approach to the supposed offenders, her frankness in bringing charges, and her love and generosity in the midst of making the accusation went a long way toward restoring the peace and rest of her people. But, most importantly, Israel's total approach here marvelously prefigures the *attitudes* which are implicit in Jesus' teaching about the discipline of errant brothers (Matthew 18:15-17). Our Lord, of course, gave a much more developed approach as He commanded three steps.

Biblical Steps of Discipline

The first is given in verse 15: "And if your brother sins, go and reprove him in private; if he listens to you, you have won your brother." This step, it seems, is the one most often neglected. Normally, when one thinks a brother or sister has sinned, he goes to another brother to "share" his concern—and then that person "shares" with another—and soon everyone knows of the alleged sinner. This norm has brought untold misery to the Body of Christ. "Sharing prayer concerns" about other people can become nothing more than a pious cloak for plain, unsanctified gossip. Jesus is explicit. If we think a fellow-believer is sinning, we are to go to him or her personally. If we do not have the moral courage to do so, then we should keep our mouths shut. How much sorrow we could avert if we followed this first step. A little more manliness would make for more saintliness.

The second step, according to verse 16, is:

> But if he does not listen to you, take one or two more with you, so that BY THE MOUTH OF TWO OR THREE WITNESSES EVERY FACT MAY BE CONFIRMED.

This step will reveal whether you are correct in your perceptions. Perhaps you have misunderstood, or perhaps you are right on. But, in any event, corroboration makes the situation clearer—and prevents gossip. If either of the first two steps is successful, you have redeemed the sinning believer and limited the scandal.

The third and final step comes in verse 17:

> And if he refuses to listen to them, tell it to the church; and if he refuses to listen even to the church, let him be to you as a Gentile and a tax-gatherer.

Here the unresponsive, unrepentant sinner is publicly separated from the church. If we must take this step, we can only do so in sorrow and tears. I believe in what Christ says. I believe it is necessary for the church of Christ to practice such discipline today. And if we follow the Lord's instructions with the care and candor and magnanimity Israel showed to its apparently sinning brothers, true *shalom* will be promoted within the church.

An Exemplary Response

Returning to the problem in Joshua, we see that the leadership of Israel modeled a godly approach to the apparently sinning brethren. Now we see in the response of the accused an equally fine model. They did not make light of the accusation. They took it seriously. The Hebrew scholar M. H. Woudstra says that the construction of these words is meant to convey excitement.[2] They responded with sincere emotion:

> Then the sons of Reuben and the sons of Gad and the half-tribe of Manasseh answered, and spoke to the heads of the families of Israel. "The Mighty One (*El*), God (*Elohim*), the Lord (*Jehovah*), the Mighty One, God, the Lord! He knows, and may Israel itself know. If it was in rebellion, or if in an unfaithful act against the Lord do not Thou save us this day! If we have built us an altar to turn away from following the Lord, or if to offer a burnt offering or grain offering on it, or if to offer sacrifices of peace offerings on it, may the Lord Himself require it" (verses 21-23, italics mine).

They said, "If what you are saying is true and we have built an altar to turn away from God, then do not save us! Destroy us! The Lord knows our heart." They affirmed that they subscribed to the same moral religious beliefs as their brothers. They affirmed the rightness of Israel's concern. But they proclaimed their innocence.

Because the two and one-half tribes did not succumb to insulted pride and sullenly refuse to speak with their accusers, the way remained open for a fair hearing of their defense, which was given in perfect clarity:

> But truly we have done this out of concern, for a reason, saying, "In time to come your sons may say to our sons, 'What have you to do with the Lord, the God of Israel? For the Lord has made the Jordan a border between us and you, you sons of Reuben and sons of Gad; you have no portion in the Lord.'" So your sons may make our sons stop fearing the Lord (verses 24, 25).

"Because of the separation," they said, "we are afraid, as the years go by, the bulk of Israel will deny us access of worship. Now let us tell you why we built the altar." Then they went on to explain that the altar was a *visual aid* to remind their sons that they must perform their sacrifices at Shiloh in Israel.

> Therefore we said, "Let us build an altar, not for burnt offering or for sacrifice; rather it shall be a witness between us and you and between our generations after us, that we are to perform the service of the Lord before Him with our burnt offerings, and with our sacrifices and with our peace offerings, that your sons may not say to our sons in time to come, 'You have no portion in the Lord.'" Therefore we said, "It shall also come about if they say this to us or to our generations in time to come, then we shall say, 'See the copy of the altar of the Lord which our fathers made, not for burnt offering or for sacrifice; rather it is a witness between us and you.'" Far be it from us that we should rebel against the Lord and turn away from following the Lord this day, by building an altar for burnt offering, for grain offering or for sacrifice, besides the altar of the Lord our God which is before His tabernacle (verses 26-29).

"We built that altar as a visual reminder that we have all the rights to worship in the land of Israel. We have solidarity with our brothers. It is exactly the opposite of what you thought." It was an incredible thing. In fact, I think the elders of Israel were amazed. They never expected that. How could they look at that altar and think anything but the worst? But it was for the best—a witness. And *shalom* came, and was perpetuated in Israel.

Peace and Rest Assured

Israel could have been destroyed; instead, their peace was enhanced. Phinehas' words in verse 31 ring with euphoria:

> Today we know that the Lord is in our midst, because you have not committed this unfaithful act against the Lord; now you have delivered the sons of Israel from the hand of the Lord.

Phinehas and his investigative committee had not been very optimistic at the beginning of that day, when they forded the Jordan and stood face to face with the leaders of the two and one-half tribes. What plausible explanation could there be for the altar, other than the sacrilege of unauthorized worship? But now they saw what it really was—a testimony and aid to the solidarity of Israel—and they were ecstatic. Of course, when they returned to the rest of Israel, the rejoicing continued (vv. 32, 33). There would be no war, but a reassured *shalom*. How good it all was. Peace, not war!

On the other side of the Jordan, there was rejoicing too. In fact, they held a little naming ceremony for their altar. Verse 34 says:

> And the sons of Reuben and the sons of Gad called the altar Witness; "for," they said, "it is a witness between us that the Lord is God."

Some men in Israel did the right thing, and thus averted catastrophe. The lessons are many for us among God's people today. Jesus says, "Blessed are the peacemakers, for they shall be called the sons of God" (Matthew 5:9). *Peacemaker* is an active word. It means far more than "peaceful"; it means those who pursue peace—even if that effort risks conflict. It means taking forthright and necessary, even difficult, steps. If He were here, our Lord would say:

> Blessed are those who do not assume the worst when they hear of the sins of another.
>
> Blessed are those who go directly to supposed sinners.
>
> Blessed are those who are frank and up-front about their concerns.
>
> Blessed are those who are loving and magnanimous in their confrontations over sin.
>
> Blessed are those who reprove their sinning brother in private.
>
> Blessed are those who go a second time to their brother with others who care.
>
> Blessed are those who will, when all else fails, tell it to the church—with tears.

These are blessed because they are "peacemakers" and "the sons of God."

"Blessed" means, essentially, *approved*. Are we approved of God? Are we those who act to bring *shalom* to God's people?

Footnotes

1. Francis A. Schaeffer, *Joshua and the Flow of Biblical History* (Downers Grove, Ill.: InterVarsity Press, 1975), p. 174.
2. Martin H. Woudstra, *The Book of Joshua* (Grand Rapids: Eerdmans, 1983), pp. 326, 327.

14

JOSHUA'S FIRST FAREWELL: Guarding Against Apostasy Joshua 23:1-16

The twenty-third chapter of Joshua gives us the first installment of Joshua's final advice to his people. He most likely gave this initial advice in Shiloh, for all the preceding action in chapters 18—22 takes place there, and it was the center of Israel's worship and administrative life.[1] He delivered the final part of his advice, which we will consider in the next chapter, in Shechem.

The text records that Joshua described himself as "old, advanced in years," and that he was. As best we can determine he was somewhere between one hundred and one hundred and ten years old (cf. 23:1 and 24:29). His greatness was unquestioned. In fact, his life bore remarkable parallels to that of the incomparable Moses. Both had a "burning bush" experience. In Joshua's case, it was with the "captain of the host" (5:13-15). Both held up a javelin at the crucial time of battle (8:26; Exodus 17:8-16). Both built an altar to the Lord (8:30; Exodus 17:15, 16). And now both will have given similar farewell addresses (cf. Deuteronomy 31, 32).[2]

This great man, realizing that death is imminent, "called," as verse 2 says, "for all Israel, for their elders and their heads and their judges, and their officers." Thus, a great crowd assembled, consisting of nearly all their leaders and many interested observers from the common multitudes. Certainly Caleb was there, aged himself, and Phinehas and the soldiers—many of whom were just beardless boys when it all began over a quarter of a century before.

At length, after the listeners had properly assembled, Joshua spoke—and what he said bore his transcending concern: *that*

Israel not apostatize, or fall away from the faith. Joshua's great fear that Israel would forsake God colored all his final words. That fear showed clearly in his mention of the "nations" (the *goyim,* the Gentiles) seven times in this final speech—though he did not use the word once in the preceding twenty-two chapters. And, as the following book of Judges sadly records, his fears were valid. Joshua's concern laid bare the truth for all of God's people—that apostasy can, and does, happen overnight.

Few people know it, but both sets of Ernest Hemingway's grandparents were committed evangelical Christians. In fact, his paternal grandparents were both graduates of Wheaton College and very close friends of D. L. Moody. His maternal grandfather was such a godly patriarchal figure that his grandchildren called him "Abba." Furthermore, one of Hemingway's uncles was a missionary to China. Yet Ernest Hemingway, after leaving his evangelical rearing in Oak Park, Illinois, became the worldwide emblem of the lost generation who said, "I live in a vacuum that is as lonely as a radio tube when the batteries are dead and there is no current to plug into"—and who took his own life.[3]

We cannot deny the fact: God's people are prone to apostasy, prone to wandering. The cases can be repeated over and over. Hannah Whitall Smith, a great guiding light of the eighteenth-century evangelical movement and author of the classic *The Christian's Secret of a Happy Life,* saw her husband leave the faith. And their son, Logan Pearsall Smith, became a famous writer and dilettante who had no use for Christianity.[4] Their daughter married Bernard Berenson, the Renaissance art critic, who lived a paradoxically animalistic, womanizing life.

And so it goes. Nearly all our country's old and honored universities began as evangelical Christian colleges. Travel to Northampton, to the site where Jonathan Edwards preached in the Great Awakening, and you will find the historic church dismissed for the summer—holding a rotating union service for a handful of attenders. Such are the realities of spiritual life. New, exciting, fresh spirituality tends to fade with amazing speed. I have seen this in men I used to look on as fellow-soldiers. Age steels no one against wandering. Some fall away in their later years after what has ostensibly been a life of service.

Joshua's final words are just as relevant today as they were those thousands of years ago; and, if taken to heart, they will hold the heart firm. What was Joshua's approach? How did he advise his people?

A Guard Against Apostasy: Remembering God's Goodness (vv. 3-5)

In verses 3-5, Joshua specifically reminded his people of what God had done for them:

> And you have seen all that the Lord your God has done to all these nations because of you, for the Lord your God is He who has been fighting for you. See, I have apportioned to you these nations which remain as an inheritance for your tribes, with all the nations which I have cut off, from the Jordan even to the Great Sea toward the setting of the sun. And the Lord your God, He shall thrust them out from before you and drive them from before you; and you shall possess their land, just as the Lord your God promised you.

They realized that God had fought for them from the very beginning, from the miraculous crossing of the Jordan, to the incredible collapse of the walls of Jericho, to the day when the sun stood still, and, as the account says, "the Lord fought for Israel" (10:14). Actually, this understanding had come upon them when they made the Exodus from Egypt and wandered in the wilderness for forty years (cf. Deuteronomy 1:30; 3:22; 20:4). Moses' charge at the crossing of the Red Sea said it all:

> Do not fear! Stand by and see the salvation of the Lord which He will accomplish for you today; for the Egyptians whom you have seen today, you will never see them again forever. The Lord will fight for you while you keep silent (Exodus 14:13, 14).

Israel experienced amazing ascendancy over their enemies. Objectively speaking, the only way anyone can account for their military dominance is that God fought for them. Moses' legion of slaves and Joshua's army of shepherds were hardly a match for either the military might of Egypt or the cities of the Canaanites, "walled to heaven." Aged Joshua knew that if his people kept in mind God's victories on their behalf and the blessings of the land He had given them, they would be less prone to wander; therefore, he began his final words with this reminder.

Recalling what God has done for us has the same keeping, preserving effect on us today. Jesus' words to the first of the seven churches in Revelation, the church in Ephesus, the church that left its first love, are, "Remember, therefore, from where you have fallen, and repent" (Revelation 2:5). Like Joshua's Israel, the Ephesians were to remember the victories and the blessings God had wrought for them. They had to bear in mind Christ's victory over sin on the cross and the glow of forgiveness which it brought to their lives. How wonderful to have their sins forgiven, and what a check against apostasy this is.

For me, the remembrance of my own salvation calls me home when I am prone to wander. I remember what it was like to come to know Christ, to know that my sins were gone, and to know the joy of calling God the Father, Abba. I remember the change He worked in my life, and that keeps me from wandering.

I remember when a young woman, a good friend of our family's—we had introduced her to Christ and I had performed her wedding—lay in a hospital the day after giving birth to a boy, whom the doctors wrongly predicted would soon die. In fact, they believed that nothing could be done for the baby and that it would be best for her or a nurse to hold the child and love him until he died. It was a dark time, but her love for Christ remained strong. She did not waver or pull away from God. She did not even emotionally apostatize. Her secret? She kept repeating phrases from Psalm 136, especially the refrain, "For His lovingkindness is everlasting."

> Give thanks to the Lord, for He is good; For His lovingkindness is everlasting. Give thanks to the God of gods, for His lovingkindness is everlasting. Give thanks to the Lord of lords, for His lovingkindness is everlasting. To Him who alone does great wonders, for His lovingkindness is everlasting (vv. 1-4).
>
> For His lovingkindness is everlasting . . . For His lovingkindness is everlasting.

Remembering what God has done for us in the past is a good defense against apostasy, and we should apply Joshua's wisdom to our own situation. If our hearts are prone to wander, prone to leave the God we love, we need to remember the victory won for us on the cross and how it was when we were forgiven through its power. We need to recall the blessings of God in our lives. But there is more, as Joshua made plain in verses 6-13.

A Further Guard Against Apostasy: Three Specific Commands for Present Living (vv. 6-13)

Joshua went on to give Israel explicit instructions for living as God's people. The first, in verse 6, was a charge to *stay under God's Word:*

> Be very firm, then, to keep and do all that is written in the book of the law of Moses, so that you may not turn aside from it to the right hand or to the left.

This is almost the same as God's charge to Joshua some twenty-five years earlier, as recorded in chapter 1, verse 7:

> Only be strong and very courageous; be careful to do according to all the law which Moses My servant commanded you; do not turn from it to the right or to the left.

Joshua charged them to keep the Word because it would prevent them from becoming secularized, assimilated into the culture. Verse 7 is very explicit about this:

> . . . in order that you may not associate with these nations, these which remain among you, or mention the name of their gods, or make anyone swear by them, or serve them, or bow down to them.

Exodus 23:13 forbade mentioning the name of false gods because it could mean the beginning of a relationship which might eventuate in walking in their ways (Micah 5:2). Swearing by a false god meant tacitly recognizing that deity; so it was forbidden (cf. Amos 8:14; Zephaniah 1:5; Jeremiah 5:7; 12:16;

and Psalm 63:12). Joshua believed that those who keep God's Word will be able to resist the worldly culture's secularizing tendencies, even in their most subtle forms. Of course, to Joshua and any other Hebrew, keeping God's Word was not just knowing it (important as that is) but obeying it. If they knew God's Word (hid it in their hearts) and then did it, they would avoid secularization.

Here it is highly significant that so many of God's servants, when asked for a "single word of advice," have emphasized being under God's Word.

> John Stott: "Get soaked in the Word. You must read the Word through once a year. As Spurgeon said, 'Your very blood must be bibline.'"
>
> Sidlow Baxter: "The making of a minister is in the private study of Scripture and secret prayer."
>
> Ray Stedman: "Learn to preach expositionally."
>
> David Howard: "Saturate yourself in the Word."
>
> Robert Coleman: "Become a man of the Book. Let everyone you work with see how much you love the Word of God."

Bowing to the authority of God's Word and obeying it will keep our heads and hearts right. A mind filled with God's Word can critically evaluate the secular society which surrounds it—and resist assimilation. A mind filled with God's Word will be a mind of wisdom. Thus, one of the vital signs of spiritual life is a regard for God's Word. When new believers join a congregation, they may not even bring a Bible for the first few weeks. As they become interested, however, they begin to look into the Word—and then there is a brand-new, shiny Bible. That Bible gradually becomes well-thumbed. When a pastor states a Bible reference in his sermon and the sanctuary fills with the rustle of pages, that church is a healthy one.

A warning sign of apostasy is a lessening of respect for the Word of God. I have seen it many, many times. When people begin to stray away or adopt a lifestyle not in keeping with the Scriptures, they simultaneously neglect God's Word. They take up a defensive agnosticism and say things like, "There are so many interpretations—who can really know what the Bible says." Sometimes their speech echoes that of the serpent to Eve in Genesis, questioning the very Word of God.

Keeping God's Word, then, was the first charge from Joshua. The second comes in verse 8, where Joshua charged his people to *cling to God:* "But you are to cling to the Lord your God, as you have done to this day." What exactly does it mean to "cling to the Lord"? Genesis 2:24, which describes marriage using the same word—"A man shall leave his father and his mother, and shall cleave (cling) to his wife; and they shall become one flesh"—gives us the idea.[5] We must cling to God in the way we cling to one another in a good marriage. It is a matter of choice and determination. Clinging to God speaks of a profound closeness which, in effect, means a new unity—a oneness. It develops from realizing how much the other cares for us and desires a relationship with us. When we see this in our Heavenly Father, we cling to Him with the deepest devotion.

The results are wonderful. First, clinging to God brings great joy. The Psalmist says in Psalm 63:7, 8,

> Thou hast been my help, and in the shadow of Thy wings I sing for joy. My soul clings to Thee; Thy right hand upholds me.

Moreover, clinging to God brings power and victory. Verses 8 and 9 give the complete picture:

> But you are to cling to the Lord your God, as you have done to this day. For the Lord has driven out great and strong nations from before you; and as for you, no man has stood before you to this day. One of your men puts to flight a thousand, for the Lord your God is He who fights for you, just as He promised you.

A soul which clings to God, enjoys a profound marriage-like unity, and thus attains joy and power is not likely to wander. But, as in marriage, cleaving belongs in the realm of the will. We must will to cling to our spouses. We must will to cling to God. Ancient Joshua urges his people with all of his heart to do so—for their souls' sake.

His third command for present living was to *love God*. Joshua phrased it beautifully in verse 11: "So take diligent heed to yourselves to love the Lord your God." Literally, it says, "take care for your very souls to love the Lord your God." The people of Israel were to make sure that they loved God for their own souls' sake. God's children are to consciously turn the whole person toward loving Him—heart and soul.

Once when a clever lawyer tried to trick Jesus and asked Him, "Teacher, which is the great commandment in the Law?" Jesus answered him,

> You shall love the Lord your God with all your heart, and with all your soul, and with all your mind. This is the great and foremost commandment. And a second is like it, "You shall love your neighbor as yourself." On these two commandments depend the whole Law and the Prophets.

The truth is: love God and you will not seek what is inconsistent with that love. Love God and you will possess Him, and He will possess you. C. S. Lewis said it all when, three weeks before his death, he wrote to an eleven-year-old girl, "If you continue to love Jesus, nothing much can go wrong with you, and I hope you may always do so."[6]

Love of God is the greatest possible guard against apostasy. If we "take diligent heed . . . to love God," we will be shielded from apostasy. In addition, it will have a similar effect on our loved ones and friends—they will be less likely to wander if our hearts are loving.

A Final Guard Against Apostasy: Keeping in Mind the Consequences (vv. 14-16)

As a last check on apostasy, Joshua reminded his people of the difference between the rewards of faithfulness and the consequences of turning away. The believer who remains firm in God leads a sublime life, as he said in verse 14:

> Now behold, today I am going the way of all the earth, and you know in all your hearts and in all your souls that not one word of all the good words which the Lord your God spoke concerning you has failed; all have been fulfilled for you, not one of them has failed.

The Israelites were to understand with all their being that not one word of God's promises had failed. We should understand that this is still true for a life of faith. Not one of His words fails. The blessings are immense for those who follow God.

However, Joshua also reminds us of the tragedy of apostasy in his very final words:

> And it shall come about that just as all the good words which the Lord your God spoke to you have come upon you, so the Lord will bring upon you all the threats, until He has destroyed you from off this good land which the Lord your God has given you. When you transgress the covenant of the Lord your God, which He commanded you, and go and serve other gods, and bow down to them, then the anger of the Lord will burn against you, and you shall perish quickly from off the good land which He has given you (vv. 15, 16).

It happened to Israel, and it individually, spiritually happens to believers today. It happened in the Hemingway family. It happened in Hannah Whitall Smith's family. It has happened to people you know. And the result of apostasy is misery—for the person, for the family, for the church.

Here, then, are the penultimate written words of one of God's greatest men. What an honored privilege to sit at his feet. His words came from his heart. He delivered them, not dispassionately, but with deep emotion. Joshua wanted to steel the Lord's people against the real threat of apostasy. How?

First, by calling to their remembrance the deliverance God had wrought in their lives. We must recall how hopeless life was without Him, and then remember the victory over sin and the ensuing *shalom* which we experienced through His work. If we do this, our spiritual fidelity will be greatly enhanced.

Second, the Lord guards His people by giving them three commands for present living: keep the Word, cling to Him, and love Him.

Last, believers are to think of the consequences of their actions. Apostasy brings misery. But fidelity brings goodness.

> Know in all your hearts and in all your souls that not one word of all the good words which the Lord your God spoke concerning you has failed; all have been fulfilled for you, not one of them has failed (v. 14).

In this first farewell speech, Joshua outlined for his people the way to stand fast in the Lord. The instructions he gave are ones that we, as God's people, must continue to follow.

Footnotes

1. E. John Hamlin, *Inheriting the Land* (Grand Rapids: Eerdmans, 1983), p. 179.
2. Martin H. Woudstra, *The Book of Joshua* (Grand Rapids: Eerdmans, 1981), p. 332.
3. Daniel Pawley, "Ernest Hemingway, Tragedy of an Evangelical," *Christianity Today,* November 23, 1984, pp. 20-22.
4. For this sad story read Logan Pearsall Smith's *Unforgotten Years* (Boston: Little, Brown and Company, 1939).
5. Hamlin, p. 187.
6. Lyle W. Dorsett and Marjorie Lamp Mead, eds., *C. S. Lewis' Letters to Children* (New York: Macmillan, 1985), p. 111.

15

JOSHUA'S FINAL FAREWELL: Choosing, Committing, Serving Joshua 24:1-33

As great as Joshua's advice at Shiloh was, and is, he had not said all he wanted to say, for he knew that his advice would only work for those whose hearts were deeply committed to God. Thus, for the sole purpose of solidifying Israel's commitment, he called a final great assembly, in the Valley of Shechem—a breath-taking setting. It was, at that time, easily the most beautiful place in all the Holy Land, and its position between Mt. Ebal and Mt. Gerizim made for the highest drama. There Joshua had constructed a great altar on Mt. Ebal and then erected ten great whitewashed stone monoliths, which bore the essence of the Law, emblazoned in red. And there he had conducted *all* of Israel's hundreds of thousands in a thunderous antiphonal chant. Those on Mt. Ebal had roared earth-shaking amens to the reading of the curses, and those on Gerizim had thundered amens to the blessings as they affirmed their commitment to keep the Law (cf. 8:30-35). To my mind, it was the most spectacular event in all the Bible, apart from some of the miracles.

In addition to this, the people of Israel also treasured the Valley of Shechem for its ancient historical associations. Some four hundred years earlier, Abraham had pitched his first tent in Palestine at Shechem; it was his first resting-place in the Promised Land. It was there that he built his first altar and there that he received his first promises about the land. His grandson, Jacob, purchased a section of land from the Shechemites and also built an altar there (Genesis 33:18-20). Later, at God's command, he had his family give him all their foreign gods and idolatrous implements and buried them under the oak in Shechem (Genesis 35:2–4). Shechem was special to Israel. "If you were to put Plymouth Rock and Yorktown and Lexington and Independence Hall together, you would not have what Shechem is to Israel."[1] Shechem had been the place of historic commitment—and now God would make it the site of Israel's great commitment.

Verse 1 of our text tells us,

> Then Joshua gathered all the tribes of Israel to Shechem, and called for the elders of Israel and for their heads and their judges and their officers; and they presented themselves before God.

Here the list is more inclusive than that for the preceding assembly, and we can well imagine that nearly all of Israel was there. Perhaps as many as a million people positioned themselves around Joshua on the slopes. They came reverently and with self-conscious gravity because "they presented themselves before God." Calvin believed that each of the people considered God to be presiding over the assembly, "and that they were not engaged in a private business, but confirming a sacred . . . compact with God himself."[2] In the midst stood ancient Joshua, now within a step of death. Though all the assembly certainly could not hear, all waited reverently for the message to come their way. And though Joshua spoke with the trembling lips of the aged, never did a man speak with more conviction. For he believed, rightly, that the future of Israel rested upon the reception of his words.

In this remarkable final speech, Joshua's evensong, we see how he brought his people to an honest, thought-through commitment to God. His words exemplify the process by which we, too, as God's people, come to and fulfill our commitment to Him.

A Preparation for Commitment: Remembering What God Has Done (vv. 2-13)

As the first step in Joshua's call to commitment, he reminded his people of how God had already blessed them. This is in perfect harmony with one of the great lessons in Joshua, where God commanded Israel to set up memorial stones in the Jordan River and in Gilgal so that they would "become a memorial to the sons of Israel forever" (4:7). God knew that remembering how He brought them miraculously across the Jordan would bolster the Israelites' spiritual health; so He commanded the stones. In keeping with this, Joshua held up four memories or "stones of remembrance" to God's people. The first, in verses 2-4, was Joshua's reminder that the creation of Israel through Abraham was solely His work. God *chose* to adopt Abraham, and thus Israel. Then, beginning at the end of verse 4 and extending through 7, Joshua set up the second stone of remembrance: the Lord's work in Israel's captivity and exodus. He made special mention here of the supernatural plagues which forced Israel's deliverance and the great miracle of the parting of the Red Sea. The third stone of remembrance comes in verses 7b-10, where Joshua told of the wilderness wanderings and how God delivered His people from the witchcraft of Balaam. And then, finally, the fourth stone (verses 11-13) was the memory of the Jordan crossing and God's dispersal of His people's enemies, as though a hornet had driven them out. Israel now occupied a land and cities for which they had not labored; God had given it to them.

As Joshua held up these "stones of remembrance" of Israel's history, the message was obvious. Israel owed its existence to the hand of God. Everything came from God. Twenty-one verbs in the first person singular dominate this short recitation of Israel's history, and all of them are God speaking. He did everything.[3] John Calvin, commenting on these verses, said he thought they were the inspiration for the lyrics of Psalm 44:1-3, and they may well be:

> God, we have heard with our ears,
> Our fathers have told us,
> The work that Thou didst in their days,
> In the days of old.
> Thou with Thine own hand didst drive out the nations;
> Then Thou didst plant them;
> Thou didst afflict the peoples,
> Then Thou didst spread them abroad.
> For by their own sword they did not possess the land;

> And their own arm did not save them;
> But Thy right hand, and Thine arm, and the light of Thy presence,
> For Thou didst favor them.

Joshua made a great, driving point to the hundreds of thousands sitting on the slopes about him: God did everything; therefore, He is a God worth committing oneself to.

This is just what our own personal "stones of remembrance" do for us. That is what those precious memories which I recorded in a previous chapter do for me. They encourage me to trust Christ with my life. A remembrance which goes back over twenty years to the birth of my first child does it every time I think of it, and I think of it often. I was in college full-time and worked full-time in a factory. My wife, Barbara, was two weeks away from delivery. Though we had saved carefully, school cost so much that, according to my calculations, I would only have about $160 when the baby came. This was not too good—the hospital cost $250 and the doctor $250. We did not know what we were going to do, and we certainly prayed. What happened is unforgettable. My wife went to the doctor for a check-up. While reading the charts the doctor, who was not a churchgoing man, noticed that I was studying for the ministry, and remarked, "We don't charge the cloth." My young wife said, "What's the cloth?" And he explained that it meant preachers. We could not believe it. We had never sought it or thought it! Then the baby came, our daughter Holly, and I had only $163. What would I do? Little did I suspect that because we came into the hospital just as the day was changing, we were charged for one less day. The bill came to $160. I had $3 left and bought Barbara flowers!

Whenever I think of that day in 1963, I realize that God did it all—and that a God who can do this can do anything. What a spur to commitment. I can trust my life with a God who can do that. That is what remembering does. And if any of us will think back in our lives, we have memories which tell us the same thing. Those memories not only keep us from wandering (as we saw in Joshua's first farewell), but they also enable commitment. Challenge yourself to think back on those things and deepen your commitment. That is God's pattern.

Confrontation with Commitment: Making the Choice to Serve (vv. 14-18)

Israel had been listening reverently to Joshua's words. The essence of what he had said had filtered back to those too distant to hear. Now, Joshua made the logical connection with these great memories of God's work by challenging the whole nation to choose commitment.

Perhaps if he was strong enough, Joshua shouted his next words (vv. 14, 15):

> Now therefore, fear the Lord and serve Him in sincerity and truth; and put away the gods which your fathers served beyond the River and in Egypt, and serve the Lord. And if it is disagreeable in your sight to serve the Lord, choose for yourselves today whom you will serve: whether the gods which your fathers served which were beyond the River, or the gods of the Amorites in whose land you are living; but as for me and my house, we will serve the Lord.

It was an extremely powerful and logically compelling challenge. If this God, who acted as He did in space, time, and history for His people, calls for commitment, then commitment becomes the only rational thing to do. Joshua's logic foreshadowed that of the Apostle Paul in Romans. Paul devoted the first eleven chapters to showing what God has done through Christ for His people, and then says in the opening verse of chapter 12:

> I urge you therefore, brethren, by the mercies of God, to present your bodies a living and holy sacrifice, acceptable to God, which is your *reasonable* (literal Greek) service of worship.

We should note that the Greek word for "reasonable" is *logikos,* from which we derive our word "logical."[4] Joshua's call, like Paul's, was the only thing that made sense in the light of who God is. Total commitment is the only thing that makes sense today if God is who He says He is.

This challenge derives its power not only from its logic, but also from the example of the man who issues it. Joshua's ethos gave his words great credibility because he had spent his life making the right choices—and all of Israel knew it. For more than a century he had "walked his talk" and this, combined with his impeccable logic, captured his people. The form of his expression added the final compelling touch: "choose for yourselves today whom you will serve . . . but as for me and my house, we will serve the Lord." "Listen! If none of you follow, it will make no difference, because I (though I am near death) will serve the Lord, and so will my house, regardless of what you do." His fierce independence added to his compelling power.

Besides its power, this challenge held urgency. He said, "choose for yourselves today." Joshua called for immediate decisions because he knew that indecision is itself a choice. A reticence to choose God equals an active choice for evil. He appealed to his people's wills because human choice makes all the difference in the world. His passion was real because he believed they had a choice—and that they were prone to choose wrongly and leave the God they loved.

The Bible represents us as we are, made in the image of God. We are not robots. We are not helplessly subject to the cause and effect arrangements of life, despite the arguments of the behaviorists. Adam chose wrongly. Abraham chose rightly. And we, like the Israelites, can choose either way. It is up to us.

We must understand that God holds absolute sovereignty. He does as He wills among men. But, from ground level, we choose—and the responsibility is ours. Not only do we choose to receive or reject Christ, we also choose the quality of our Christian life. A year after I came to know Christ as a young teenager, I was faced with Paul's impeccable logic: if Christ had done all for me, then there was only one *logical* way to live—with total commitment. As best I could at my age, I gave everything to Him. My wife, as a sophomore in high school, did the same thing. The choices we made determined the quality and course of our spiritual lives. We are who we are today, and we do what we are doing, because of a choice made years ago.

When faced with the Scriptures, we cannot doubt that they call *everyone* to total commitment to God. I believe that most of us ought to be able to point to a time when we gave our lives totally to Christ. If we cannot do this, then we should at least be able to recall the stage in our lives when this yielding took place. If you are a new Christian, it is the only logical thing to do. If you have never given yourself completely to God, then why not today?

Joshua's challenge to make that full commitment, that choice for service, fell on Israel with the force of a sledgehammer, and they thundered their affirmative. No doubt the record of it in verses 16-18 was shouted by Israel's leaders, and then a roar of affirmation spread across the vast throng.

> And the people answered and said, "Far be it from us that we should forsake the Lord to serve other gods; for the Lord our God is He who brought us and our fathers up out of the land of Egypt, from the house of bondage, and who did these great signs in our sight and preserved us through all the way in which we went and among all the peoples through whose midst we passed. And the Lord drove out from before us all the peoples, even the Amorites who lived in the land. We also will serve the Lord, for He is our God."

One would expect that this great response would have thrilled aged Joshua—and that now his soul could depart in peace. But it was not so.

Authentication of Commitment: Counting the Cost and Taking Responsibility (vv. 19-24)

Joshua was uneasy with his people's enthusiastic response. To him it seemed too glib, too ready. After all, he remembered their past fickleness far too well. He had seen one zealous resolution after another evaporate in the heat of life. John Calvin, a leader not unlike Joshua, insightfully comments:

> But there is no doubt that his tongue was guided by the inspiration of the Spirit. . . . For when the Lord brings a man under his authority, they are usually willing enough to profess zeal for piety, though they would instantly fall away from it. Thus they built without a foundation. This happens because they neither distrust their own weakness so much as they ought, nor consider how difficult it is to bind themselves wholly to the Lord.[5]

Joshua knew, as has every experienced believer from every age, that it is difficult to follow God fully. He knew that sentimental, romantic resolutions made in the emotion of the moment will not endure.

Joshua did not go for smooth, airy resolve; so he issued two warnings to the multitudes. The first warning is in verses 19, 20:

> Then Joshua said to the people, "You will not be able to serve the Lord, for He is a holy God. He is a jealous God; He will not forgive your transgressions or your sins. If you forsake the Lord and serve foreign gods, then He will turn and do you harm and consume you after He has done good to you."

Joshua did not mean that it is impossible to serve the Lord; rather he meant that it cannot be done with shallow resolve. His people must understand that because their holy God dwells in unapproachable sanctity, He cannot have unholy servants. Moreover, because He wants to pour His love into them, He will tolerate no rivals. Continued unrepentant sin will leave them unforgiven. Joshua's warning foreshadows exactly what Jesus, the ultimate Joshua, did with His would-be followers:

> And a certain scribe came and said to Him, "Teacher, I will follow You wherever You go." And Jesus said to him, "The foxes have holes, and the birds of the air have nests; but the Son of Man has nowhere to lay His head" (Matthew 8:19, 20).
>
> Now great multitudes were going along with Him; and He turned and said to them . . . "Whoever does not carry his own cross and come after Me cannot be My disciple. For which of you, when he wants to build a tower, does not first sit down and calculate the cost, to see if he has enough to complete it?" (Luke 14:25, 27, 28).

Joshua had sounded his warning, and what was the result? He must have shown pleasure at the answer. Verse 21: "And the people said to Joshua, 'We will serve the Lord our God and we will obey His voice.'"

The second warning and response is in verses 22-24:

> And Joshua said to the people, "You are witnesses against yourselves that you have chosen for yourselves the Lord, to serve Him." And they said, "We are witnesses." "Now therefore, put away the foreign gods which are in your midst, and incline your hearts to the Lord, the God of Israel." And the people said to Joshua, "We will serve the Lord our God and we will obey His voice."

When Joshua swore them in as witnesses against themselves, it meant that they had written their own sentence if they became unfaithful. Their thunderous affirmation, "We are witnesses," signaled that they took full responsibility for their actions. Their commitment to serve the Lord was now far more intelligent and deeper than when first affirmed—and Joshua was pleased. The fact is, as Judges 2:7 tells us,

> And the people served the Lord all the days of Joshua, and all the days of the elders who survived Joshua, who had seen all the great work of the Lord which He had done for Israel (Judges 2:10).

Joshua's challenge to commitment was a vast success!

From this we learn that no true seeker will be repelled when we emphasize the difficulty of the Way. God's Word tells us that total commitment to Him is the only *logical* way to live our Christianity. When we consider who God is and what He has done in history, and for us personally, any other choice is illogical, irrational. But the Word says that it is not easy to follow the Lord. All commitments should be made in the light of these twin truths.

Confirmation of Commitment: Marking the Covenant (vv. 25-31)

The flow of Joshua's challenge had gone from bringing to mind what God had done for them to issuing the bold challenge to testing their sincerity. It was time to officially commemorate his people's commitment.

Recall the mystic setting between the slopes of Ebal and Gerizim: myriads of people filled the horizon, and ancient Joshua stood beside the altar, with its majestic white stones bearing testimony to the Law. In this overwhelming moment, Joshua solemnized his people's commitment (verses 25-28):

> So Joshua made a covenant with the people that day, and made for them a statute and an ordinance in Shechem. And Joshua wrote these words in the book of the Law of God; and he took a large stone and set it up there under the oak that was by the sanctuary of the Lord. And Joshua said to all the people, "Behold, this stone shall be for a witness against us, for it has heard all the words of the Lord which He spoke to us; thus it shall be for a witness against you, lest you deny your God." Then Joshua dismissed the people, each to his inheritance.

Now Israel had another great "stone of remembrance." Their history during the last twenty-five years could almost be told by the stones of remembrance. The twin piles of twelve stones in the Jordan and at Gilgal reminded them of their miraculous placement in the Promised Land. The stone mounds over the kings of Jericho and Ai recalled God's righteous judgment. The ten monoliths in Shechem spoke of their commitment to the Law; and now the stone under the oak (perhaps the same oak of Abraham and Jacob) called to mind their official thrice-repeated commitment to serve the Lord.

It was done. Joshua's life-mission was complete. Verses 29-31 tell us:

> And it came about after these things that Joshua the son of Nun, the servant of the Lord, died, being one hundred and ten years old. And they buried him in the territory of his inheritance in Timnath-serah, which is in the hill country of Ephraim, on the north of Mount Gaash. And Israel served the Lord all the days of Joshua and all the days of the elders who survived Joshua, and had known all the deeds of the Lord which He had done for Israel.

What is the message for us? Simply this: we must choose for ourselves today whom we will serve. If you are not a Christian, you must choose Christ today.

> Your choice is not a piece of theatre. You are not a thistledown in the wind. There are good and sufficient reasons in

> history to know that this is a choice you should make, and you are called upon to make it. Choose once and for all justification.[6]

The Scriptures say that today is the day to choose: "Now is the day of salvation."

> I pleaded for time to be given.
> He said: "Is it hard to decide?
> It will not seem so hard in heaven
> To have followed the steps of your Guide."
> (George MacDonald)

If you choose Christ, eternity will reveal it is the greatest choice you ever made. Why not choose Christ now?

And if we are Christians who have made the once-for-all choice of knowing Christ, we must remember that our choices do not end. We must choose to commit all of our lives to Him. Paul says it is the only logical thing to do. It is your "reasonable service of worship."

Footnotes

1. Clarence Macartney, *The Greatest Texts of the Bible* (Nashville: Abingdon, 1947), pp. 74, 75.
2. John Calvin, *Commentaries on the Book of Joshua* (Grand Rapids: Baker, 1984), p. 271.
3. E. John Hamlin, *Inheriting the Land* (Grand Rapids: Eerdmans, 1983), p. 193.
4. C. E. B. Cranfield, *Romans,* ICC, Vol. 2 (Edinburgh: T & T Clark, 1975), pp. 603-605.
5. Calvin, p. 276.
6. Francis A. Schaeffer, *Joshua and the Flow of Biblical History* (Downers Grove, Ill.: InterVarsity Press, 1975), p. 214.

APPENDIX
Joshua 10—20—Battle Histories and Land Settlements

I. The southern campaign (chapter 10)
II. The northern campaign (chapter 11)
III. The list of defeated kings (chapter 12)
IV. The dividing of the land (chapters 13—21)
  A. The method of division (13:1—14:5)
  B. Caleb's portion (14:6-15)
  C. The portion of Judah (15:1-63)
  D. The portion of the Joseph tribes (16:1—17:18
  E. The portions of the remaining seven tribes (18:1—19:51)
  F. The cities of refuge (20:1-9)
  G. The Levitical cities (21:1-45)

WORKS CITED

St. Anselm. *Cur Deus Homo*. Vol. X. Library of Christian Classics.

Baldwin, E. M. *Henrietta Mears and How She Did It*. Regal, n.d.

Blaikie, William Garden. *The Book of Joshua*. A. C. Armstrong and Sons, 1903.

Boling, Robert G., and G. Ernest Wright. *Joshua*. The Anchor Bible Series. Doubleday, 1982.

Bright, John. *The Interpreter's Bible*. Vol. 2. Abingdon, 1953.

Butler, Trent C. *Word Biblical Commentary: Joshua*. Word, 1983.

Calvin, John. *Commentaries on the Book of Joshua*. Trans. Henry Beveridge. Baker, 1984.

Claypool, John R. *The Preaching Event*. Word, 1980.

Cranfield, C. E. B. *Romans*, ICC. T & T Clark, 1975.

Davis, John J. *Conquest and Crisis: Studies in Joshua, Judges, and Ruth*. Baker, 1976.

Dorsett, Lyle W., and Marjorie Lamp Mead, eds. *C. S. Lewis' Letters to Children*. Macmillan, 1985.

Douglas, J. D., ed. *The New Bible Dictionary*. Eerdmans, 1962.

Giesler, Norman L. *The Christian Love Ethic*. Zondervan, 1979.

Ginzberg, Louis. *The Legends of the Jews*. Vol. 4. The Jewish Publication Society, 1954.

Hamlin, E. John. *Inheriting the Land*. Eerdmans, 1983.

Hastings, James, ed. *The Great Men and Women of the Bible, Moses—Samson*. Vol. II. T & T Clark, 1914.

Hopkins, Hugh Evan. *Charles Simeon of Cambridge*. Eerdmans, 1977.

Keil, C. F., and F. Delitzsch. *Joshua, Judges, Ruth*. Eerdmans, 1963.

Kuyper, Abraham. *Women of the Old Testament*. Zondervan, 1961.

Lewis, C. S. *The Lion, the Witch, and the Wardrobe*. Collins, 1974.

Macartney, Clarence. *The Greatest Texts of the Bible*. Abingdon, 1947.

_________. *Macartney's Illustrations*. Abingdon, 1946.

Maclaren, Alexander. *Expositions of Holy Scripture: Deuteronomy, Joshua*. Vol. 2. Baker, 1974.

Matthew Henry's Commentary on the Whole Bible. Vol. 2 Revell, n.d.

Nicoll, W. Robertson. *The Expositor's Bible*. A. C. Armstrong and Sons, 1903.

Orr, James, ed. *The International Standard Bible Encyclopedia*. Vol. 1. Eerdmans, 1939.

Pawley, Daniel. "Ernest Hemingway, Tragedy of an Evangelical." *Christianity Today*, November 23, 1984, pp. 20-22.

Sanders, J. Oswald. *Spiritual Leadership*. Moody, 1967.

Sangster, Paul. *Doctor Sangster*. Epworth Press, 1962.

Schaeffer, Francis A. *Joshua and the Flow of Biblical History*. InterVarsity Press, 1975.

Schmidt, Dietmer. *Pastor Niemoller*. Trans. Lawrence Wilson. Doubleday, 1959.

Smith, Logan Pearsall. *Unforgotten Years*. Little, Brown and Company, 1939.

Spurgeon, Charles. *The Metropolitan Tabernacle Pulpit*. Vol. 14. Pilgrim Publications, 1970.

Von Rad, Gerhard. *Old Testament Theology*. Vol. 1. Trans. D. M. G. Stalker. Harper & Row, 1962.

Woudstra, M. H. *The Book of Joshua*. Eerdmans, 1981.

Zartel, Adam. "Has Joshua's Altar Been Found at Mount Ebal?" *Biblical Archaeological Review* 22:1 (Jan.-Feb. 1985), pp. 26-43.